Reconstruction

Lucent Library of Black History

Other titles in this series:

Reconstruction

Lucent Library of Black History

Michael V. Uschan

LUCENT BOOKS

A part of Gale, Cengage Learning

GALE
CENGAGE Learning·

Detroit • New York • San Francisco • New Haven, Conn • Waterville, Maine • London

© 2008 Gale, a part of Cengage Learning

For more information, contact
Lucent Books
27500 Drake Rd.
Farmington Hills, MI 48331-3535
Or you can visit our Internet site at gale.cengage.com

LIBRARY OF CONGRESS CATALOGING-IN-PUBLICATION DATA

Uschan, Michael V., 1948–
  Reconstruction / by Michael V. Uschan.
      p. cm. — (Lucent library of Black history)
  Includes bibliographical references and index.
  ISBN 978-1-4205-0009-7 (hardcover)
  1. African Americans—History—1863-1877—Juvenile literature. 2. Reconstruction (U.S. history, 1865-1877)—Juvenile literature. 3. African Americans—Civil rights—Southern States—History—19th century—Juvenile literature. 4. African Americans—Southern States—Social conditions—19th century—Juvenile literature. I. Title.
  E185.2.U83 2008
  973.8—dc22   2007041352

ISBN-10: 1-4205-0009-0

Printed in the United States of America
  2 3 4 5 6 7 12 11 10 09 08

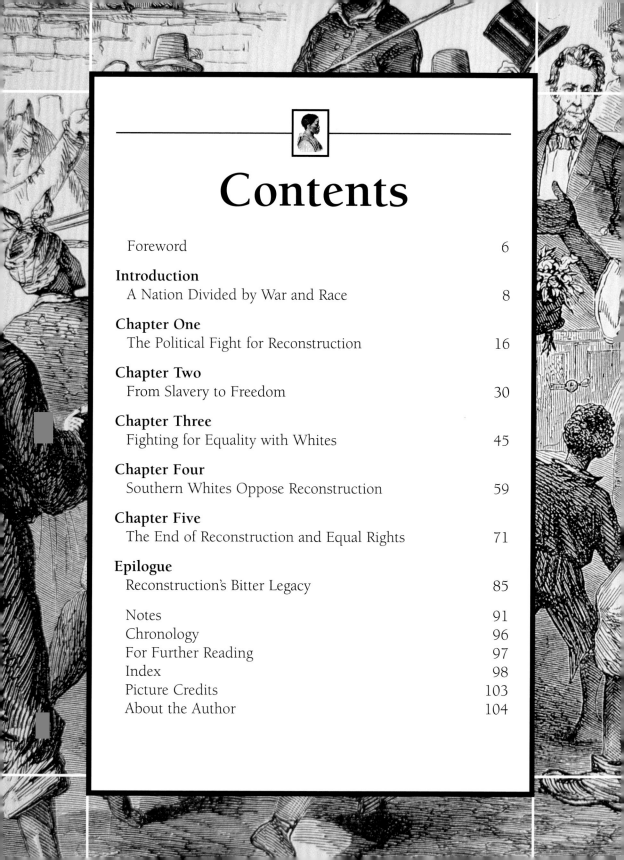

Contents

Foreword

It has been more than 500 years since Africans were first brought to the New World in shackles, and over 140 years since slavery was formally abolished in the United States. Over 50 years have passed since the fallacy of "separate but equal" was obliterated in the American courts, and some 40 years since the watershed Civil Rights Act of 1965 guaranteed the rights and liberties of all Americans, especially those of color. Over time, these changes have become celebrated landmarks in American history. In the twenty-first century, African American men and women are politicians, judges, diplomats, professors, deans, doctors, artists, athletes, business owners, and home owners. For many, the scars of the past have melted away in the opportunities that have been found in contemporary society. Observers such as Peter N. Kirsanow, who sits on the U.S. Commission of Civil Rights, point to these accomplishments and conclude, "The growing black middle class may be viewed as proof that most of the civil rights battles have been won."

In spite of these legal victories, however, prejudice and inequality have persisted in American society. In 2003, African Americans comprised just 12 percent of the nation's population, yet accounted for 44 percent of its prison inmates and 24 percent of its poor. Racially motivated hate crimes continue to appear on the pages of major newspapers in many American cities. Furthermore, many African Americans still experience either overt or muted racism in their daily lives. A 1996 study undertaken by Professor Nancy Krieger of the Harvard School of Public Health, for example, found that 80 percent of the African American participants reported having experienced racial discrimination in one or more settings, including at work or school, applying for housing and medical care, from the police or in the courts, and on the street or in a public setting.

It is for these reasons that many believe the struggle for racial equality and justice is far from over. These episodes of discrimi-

6

nation threaten to shatter the illusion that America has completely overcome its racist past, causing many black Americans to become increasingly frustrated and confused. Scholar and writer Ellis Cose has described this splintered state in the following way: "I have done everything I was supposed to do. I have stayed out of trouble with the law, gone to the right schools, and worked myself nearly to death. What more do they want? Why in God's name won't they accept me as a full human being?" For Cose and others, the struggle for equality and justice has yet to be fully achieved.

In many subtle yet important ways the traumatic experiences of slavery and segregation continue to inform the way race is discussed and experienced in the twenty-first century. Indeed, it is possible that America will always grapple with the fallout from its distressing past. Ulric Haynes, dean of the Hofstra University School of Business has said, "Perhaps race will always matter, given the historical circumstances under which we came to this country." But studying this past and understanding how it contributes to present-day dialogues about race and history in America is a critical component of contemporary education. To this end, the Lucent Library of Black History offers a thorough look at the experiences that have shaped the black community and the American people as a whole. Annotated bibliographies provide readers with ideas for further research, while fully documented primary and secondary source quotations enhance the text. Each book in the series explores a different episode of black history; together they provide students with a wealth of information as well as launching points for further study and discussion.

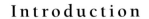

A Nation Divided by War and Race

The Declaration of Independence is one of the most important documents in U.S. history. Representatives of all thirteen British colonies approved the declaration on July 4, 1776, to explain why they were seeking their freedom from England in the American Revolution. It boldly declared that colonists had basic rights no one could deny them, not even the British king. It also claimed that everyone had the same rights and privileges. Both political principles were radical concepts in an age in which kings and other members of royal families ruled nations and had greater rights than other citizens. The Declaration's most famous words are these: "We hold these truths to be self-evident, that all men are created equal, that they are endowed by their Creator with certain unalienable Rights, that among these are Life, Liberty and the pursuit of happiness."[1]

Today those powerful promises of freedom and equality are considered the philosophical foundation that has made the United States a great nation. But in 1776 and for another hundred years afterward, those sacred pledges were true only for white people, because millions of African Americans lived as slaves. It was not until the Civil War and the Reconstruction era that followed it that the United States finally tried to extend those promises to blacks.

Slavery in the United States

Legalized slavery in the United States began in 1619 when a Dutch ship landed in Virginia with twenty blacks who were soon sold as slaves. They arrived twelve years after Virginia became the first British colony. England in the next century established a dozen more colonies, and the practice of using slaves as cheap labor spread to them all.

After the United States defeated England in the American Revolution, it allowed slavery to continue even though the practice violated principles in the Declaration of Independence and five

Though freedom was declared to "all citizens" in the Constitution, this statement did not include the nation's slaves. Even George Washington, the nation's first president, owned slaves.

thousand African American soldiers, both free and slave, had helped the colonies win their freedom. The 1790 federal census showed the United States had 697,681 slaves; by 1810 that number had risen to 1.2 million and by 1860 to nearly 4 million. Among the nation's slave owners were key figures who helped found the nation, including George Washington and Thomas Jefferson, both of whom owned slaves while serving as president.

Despite its widespread acceptance, many people in the eighteenth and nineteenth centuries began to believe slavery was wrong. Even slave owners like Jefferson had mixed feelings about the practice. Jefferson authored the Declaration of Independence, and his original draft included a condemnation of slavery. Although that statement was deleted at the insistence of representatives from colonies who backed slavery, Jefferson once predicted that "nothing is more certainly written in the Book of Fate than that this people [African Americans] shall be free."[2]

When the states met in 1787 to write the U.S. Constitution, representatives from Northern states tried to declare slavery illegal. The attempt was bitterly opposed by Southern states, which depended on the cheap labor slavery provided for agriculture. Northern states allowed slavery to continue because they feared Southerners would reject any constitution that outlawed slavery and maybe even break away to start a new country.

Antislavery Sentiment Grows

Political and social divisions between north and south widened during the first half of the nineteenth century as more Northerners began to believe slavery was immoral. By 1804 every Northern state had outlawed slavery within its borders. Those states rejected the philosophical underpinning of slavery, which was that blacks were racially inferior and whites could own and sell blacks like they did animals such as cows or horses.

Frederick Douglass was born into slavery in Maryland in 1818. After escaping to New York, where slavery was illegal, he became one of the leaders of the movement to abolish slavery. In a speech, Douglass described once how degrading it was to be a slave:

The condition of a slave is simply that of the brute beast. He is a piece of property—a marketable commodity, in the lan-

Former slave and abolitionist Frederick Douglass likened a slave's life as no better than a horse's.

guage of the law, to be bought or sold at the will and caprice of the master who claims him to be his property; he is spoke of, thought of, and treated as property. His own good, his conscience, his intellect, his affections are all set aside by the master. The will and the wishes of the master are the law of the slave. He is as much a piece of property as a horse. If he is fed, he is fed because he is property. If he is clothed, it is with a view to the increase of his value as property.[3]

One of the most inhumane aspects of slavery was that slave sales often separated families. Josiah Henson, who in 1830 escaped to freedom in Canada from Maryland, wrote in his autobiography how painful it was for his mother to watch when he and his brothers and sisters were sold at an auction: "My brothers and sisters were bid off first while my mother, paralyzed by grief held me by the hand. [Then] I was offered to the assembled purchasers [and] I heard her sob out, 'Oh, lord Jesus, how long, how long shall I suffer this way?' I must have been then between five and six years old. I seem to see and hear my poor weeping mother now."[4]

Such injustice led many Northern whites to oppose slavery, including Abraham Lincoln, a lawyer from Illinois. Lincoln once said he hated slavery because it violated the "definitions and axioms of free society" that Jefferson had penned in the Declaration of Independence. Lincoln once claimed that "as a nation we began by declaring that 'all men are created equal.' We now practically read it, 'all men are created equal, except Negroes.'"[5] The growing antislavery sentiment in the North in 1860 helped Lincoln win the Republican Party's nomination for president. In voting on November 6, Lincoln won with 180 electoral votes, 57 more than the combined total of his three challengers.

Lincoln in 1858 had predicted that slavery threatened the nation's continued existence. "A house divided against itself," he said in a speech, "cannot stand. I believe this government cannot endure permanently half slave and half free."[6] His election made that prophecy come true.

The Civil War

Southern states began seceding from the United States after Lincoln was elected because they feared he would try to abolish slavery. South Carolina was the first, on December 20, 1860. By the time Lincoln was inaugurated as the nation's sixteenth president on March 4, 1861, Alabama, Florida, Georgia, Louisiana, Mississippi, and Texas had joined South Carolina to form the Confederate States of America. Arkansas, North Carolina, Tennessee, and Virginia also left for the Confederacy.

In his inaugural address on March 4, 1861, Lincoln asked the rebellious states to return and vowed he would not end slavery. Said Lincoln, "I have no purpose, directly or indirectly, to interfere with the institution of slavery in the states where it exists. I believe I have no right to do so and I have no inclination to do so."[7] His promise went unheeded. The Civil War began a month later on April 12 when soldiers for the Confederate States began firing cannons at Fort Sumter, a U.S. military facility located on an island in the harbor of Charleston, South Carolina.

The nation's bloodiest and most terrible war would divide the nation until April 9, 1865, when Confederate general Robert E. Lee surrendered to Union general Ulysses S. Grant at Appomattox Courthouse in Virginia. The four years of fighting took the lives of 360,222 soldiers who fought for the North and 258,000 who battled for the South.

Lincoln's purpose at the start of the conflict had not been to free slaves but to prevent the nation from being permanently

Robert E. Lee (left) surrenders to Ulysses S. Grant, officially ending the Civil War.

divided. His attitude changed during the war. As the Union army captured Southern territory, it gained control of thousands of slaves, and thousands more flocked to Union areas to escape bondage. Lincoln realized then that freeing them was the right thing to do. He also came to believe that Union soldiers needed a higher purpose to motivate them to fight and win the brutal war. Said Lincoln of his change of heart: "The moment came when I felt that slavery must die that the nation might live."[8]

The president on September 23, 1862, announced his Emancipation Proclamation. The proclamation, which would take effect on January 1, 1863, granted freedom to slaves in the Confederacy. Although the proclamation would have no real effect until the Union defeated the Confederacy, a Northern victory by then was inevitable, and the proclamation meant that slavery would soon end for millions of African Americans.

Lincoln also began planning the peace that would follow the war. The president already knew that his most important peacetime job was to reunite North and South. This task became known as Reconstruction, because it entailed rebuilding the shattered political and social ties between the warring states so that they could once again function as one, united nation. But Reconstruction would also entail a second task, one that would prove to be much more difficult to accomplish than bringing Southern states back into the Union. And that was to figure out what to do with the 3.5 million slaves the North had freed with its victory.

A Question of Race

When the war ended, people on both sides of the conflict realized the necessity of reuniting the states. However, there was a strong division of opinion over how to treat the freed slaves. In *Reconstruction: The Ending of the Civil War*, historian Avery Craven explained that there were many unanswered questions about what rights the freed slaves should have and what position they should have in society. Wrote Craven: "When the fighting ended and slavery was abolished, there remained a race problem to be faced and solved. Until the Negro's place in American life was fixed, the war was not over. In its brutal way slavery had met that problem. Now the victorious North must assume responsibility [for the freed slaves]."[9]

There was a race problem because the freed slaves were black. Many Southerners and some Northerners, even those who opposed slavery, thought African Americans should remain second-class citizens even after blacks were freed. They did not believe blacks should have legal rights that other citizens enjoyed, such as being able to vote. Other people, however, argued that blacks deserved equality with whites and should have all the rights of white citizens. When the war ended and slavery was abolished, the nation had to learn new ways to treat blacks.

The struggle over what place the freed slaves should have in U.S. society made this second Reconstruction task much more difficult to accomplish than merely accepting the defeated Southern states back into the Union. It led to a political and social battle throughout the Reconstruction era. This battle was often accompanied by violence against black men, women, and children who were trying to make a new and better life for themselves after being freed from slavery.

The Work Had Just Begun

When the Civil War ended slavery, people who had fought to abolish it were almost as joyful as those who were freed. Frederick Douglass was one of them. In the decades leading up to the war, Douglass had worked tirelessly to end slavery. But when his goal was finally realized, Douglass knew that the fight to bring equality to blacks had not ended. He said, "Verily, the work does not end with the abolition of slavery, but only begins."[10] Douglass understood that the freed slaves would not be truly free until they enjoyed all the rights other U.S. citizens had. This was a task that many people, both black and white, tried to accomplish during the Reconstruction era.

Chapter One

The Political Fight for Reconstruction

Abraham Lincoln in 1864 won a second term as president. In his inaugural speech on March 4, 1865, Lincoln promised to welcome Southerners back into the Union once the Civil War ended. He closed his speech with these words: "With malice toward none, with charity for all, with firmness in the right as God gives us to see the right, let us strive on to finish the work we are in, to bind up the nation's wounds [and] to do all which may achieve and cherish a just and lasting peace among ourselves and with all nations."[11]

The Union finished the work Lincoln mentioned—winning the war—on April 9, 1865, when the Confederacy surrendered. It was now time for Lincoln to rebuild the shattered nation through Reconstruction.

Conflicting Reconstruction Plans

As Lincoln had stated in his inaugural address, his main peacetime goal was to bring the rebellious states back into the Union, not to seek revenge on Southerners for starting the war. Lincoln had begun that process on December 8, 1863, when he announced his Proclamation of Amnesty and Reconstruction. He offered to pardon Confederate soldiers who fought against the Union and restore their property if they would swear loyalty to the nation and agree to end slavery. His plan allowed Confederate states to be readmitted to the Union after 10 percent of the total of their 1860 voters had signed a loyalty oath.

Some Republican members of Congress believed Lincoln's plan was too lenient and that Congress, not the president, had the power to conduct Reconstruction. Representative Thaddeus Stevens stated their position by saying, "The future condition of the conquered power depends on the will of the conquerors. Congress must create States and declare when they are entitled to be represented."[12] Congressmen like Stevens became known as Radical Republicans because their plan was more radical than Lincoln's.

Radical Republicans in 1864 passed the Wade-Davis Act, which required a majority of voters in Southern states to swear allegiance before their states could be readmitted. It also prohibited many former Confederates from voting and demanded that blacks be able to vote and have other rights to make them equal to whites. Congress passed the bill July 8, 1864, but it never became law because Lincoln refused to sign it.

It was the beginning of a battle between Congress and the office of the president over Reconstruction. However, there would soon be a new president for Congress to fight.

"Grind Down the Traitors in the Dust!"

Lincoln on April 14, 1865, went to Ford's Theater in the nation's capital to watch the play *Our American Cousin*. The president, his wife, Mary, and several friends were watching the play when the door leading into their theater box was opened unexpectedly. A man entered, stepped quickly behind the seated president, and shot Lincoln once in the back of the head. The assassin leaped to the stage below, where he shouted, *"Sic semper tyrannis!"* [Latin for "thus be it ever to tyrants"] and, "The South is avenged!"[13] before he ran out of the theater. Lincoln died the next morning.

The man who shot Lincoln was John Wilkes Booth, a famous actor born in Maryland who was angry the Confederacy had been defeated. His savage act made Lincoln the first president ever assassinated. It also helped shape the course of Civil War Reconstruction by making Radical Republicans more committed than

John Wilkes Booth aims his pistol to assassinate Abraham Lincoln at Ford's Theater.

ever to treat the defeated Confederacy harshly. "Grind down the traitors. Grind the traitors in the dust!"[14] was the response of Representative Stevens to the assassination.

If Lincoln had lived, the popular president might have been able to convince his fellow Republicans to temper their treatment of the South. But he was succeeded by Vice President Andrew Johnson, a Democrat who was unpopular with Republicans and who became hated when he tried to carry out Lincoln's Reconstruction plan.

Johnson had represented Tennessee when the Civil War began and was the only U.S. senator from a Confederate state who remained loyal to the Union. Johnson had once owned slaves but now supported abolition. However, he sympathized with Southerners and shared similar racial views on blacks—Johnson believed blacks were inferior and did not think they should vote or hold public office. He once stated that "White men alone must manage the South."[15]

That belief put him at odds with Radical Republicans, who wanted to give blacks equal status with whites. Johnson, however, would have the first chance at creating Reconstruction. Congress had ended its session in March 1865 and would not reconvene until December.

The Battle Begins

Johnson quickly tried to bring Confederate states back into the Union. Before they could be readmitted, each state had to approve the Thirteenth Amendment to the U.S. Constitution, which abolished slavery. The states also had to have 10 percent of their voters sign a loyalty oath; renounce their decision to secede; and agree to not use federal funds for Confederate war debts. Louisiana, Virginia, Tennessee, and Arkansas began taking those steps when Union forces won control of them while the war was still going on. Johnson quickly accepted them back into the Union and then initiated the process in other rebel states.

Thousands of Union prisoners died due to the poor conditions at the Andersonville prison camp in Georgia.

The new president gave blanket amnesty to almost every former Confederate military and political leader. A handful of soldiers were imprisoned for war crimes, but the only important officer who was executed was Henry Wirz, who had commanded Georgia's infamous Andersonville prison. More than ten thousand Union prisoners died at Andersonville due to lack of decent food, shelter, and medical care. Confederate president Jefferson Davis was the only high-ranking civilian official imprisoned for any length of time and he was incarcerated for two years. Johnson also returned land and other property to Confederates after they swore loyalty to the Union. By December 1865 Johnson declared that Reconstruction was almost complete because every state except Texas had met the requirements for being readmitted to the Union.

Johnson's lenient Reconstruction policy, however, had emboldened Southerners to try to deny freed slaves their rights as citizens. Confederate states during the summer and fall of 1865 enacted so-called black codes. These codes prohibited blacks from voting, carrying weapons to protect themselves, or working many types of jobs. Some codes created what seemed to be a new form of slavery by allowing blacks imprisoned for vagrancy or other crimes to be forced to work for whites who paid their fines. After South Carolina's General Assembly ratified its black code, the Colored People's Convention of the State of South Carolina met to protest the measures. The group, which represented South Carolina blacks, issued a statement that said they just wanted to be treated fairly: "We have resolved to come forward, and, like MEN, speak and act for ourselves. We ask for no special privileges or favors. We ask only for even-handed Justice. We simply ask that we shall be recognized as men."[16]

By the time Congress convened in December, all-white racist governments once again ruled the South. The former slaves were technically free but still living in political and social bondage.

The Radicals Revolt

Radical Republicans began working immediately to undo what historians now call Presidential Reconstruction. Their first act of defiance was to refuse to seat congressmen from states that Johnson had readmitted to the Union. The states included Johnson's

Frederick Douglass Lectures the President

On February 7, 1866, Frederick Douglass led a delegation of African Americans who met with President Andrew Johnson in the White House. The delegation asked the president to support voting rights for blacks because it was the only way they could have equality with whites. When Johnson refused, Douglass wrote the president to explain why that right was so important. Argued Douglass:

> Can it be that you recommend a policy [denying blacks the vote] which would arm the strong and cast down the defenceless? Can you, by any possibility of reasoning, regard this as just, fair, or wise? Experience proves that those are most abused who can be abused with the greatest impunity. Men are whipped oftenest who are whipped easiest. Peace between races is not secured by degrading one race and exalting another; by giving power to one race and withholding it from another, but by maintaining a state of equal justice between all classes.

Frederick Douglass, *Autobiographies: Narrative of the Life of Frederick Douglass, an American Slave.* New York: Library of America, 1984, p. 822.

home state of Tennessee, which caused Representative James Brooks to ask, "If Tennessee is not in the Union, by what right does the president of the United States usurp a place in the White House?"[17] Brooks and other Republicans scorned Johnson, and Brooks was trying to imply that Johnson actually had no right to serve as president because his home state had not been officially readmitted to the Union. The Republican action marked the beginning of a political war between Congress and the president that would last more than two years.

Radical Republicans opposed Presidential Reconstruction for two main reasons. The first was that congressmen believed they, and not the president, had the power to carry out this important task. The second was that Johnson had allowed Confederate states to deny blacks rights they were entitled to as citizens. Even Lincoln, who had favored a more lenient attitude toward the defeated Southern states, had wanted that for blacks. Not long before Lincoln died, he said, "the restoration of the Rebel States must rest upon the civil and political equality of both races."[18]

Lincoln, however, had disagreed with radicals on whether all freed slaves should be able to vote. In his final speech on April 11, Lincoln said, "I would myself prefer that it [the right to vote] were now conferred on the very intelligent, and on those who serve our cause as soldiers."[19] Lincoln was referring to the more educated blacks as well as the 180,000 who fought for the Union during the Civil War. Radical Republicans like Massachusetts senator Charles Sumner believed it was proper to extend the vote to black males—women of any race did not get the right to vote until the Nineteenth Amendment to the Constitution took effect in 1920. Sumner even claimed that this right was the keystone to any progress for freed slaves: "This is the great guarantee without which all other guarantees will fail. This is the sole solution of our present troubles and anxieties."[20] To ensure that equality, Radical Republicans had to directly oppose the president, who did not want blacks to vote.

Congress Battles the President

The political fight between Congress and the president began on January 5, 1866, when Illinois senator Lyman Trumbull introduced two bills. One bill extended the life of the Freedmen's Bureau, an entity Lincoln had created to provide food, shelter, and medical care to freed slaves in areas the Union army captured during the Civil War. The second was the Civil Rights Bill.

The Civil Rights Bill sought to overturn the black codes by making sure that blacks enjoyed all the rights white U.S. citizens had. Trumbull, a respected but moderate Republican, claimed blacks could not be truly considered free if "laws are to be enacted and enforced depriving persons of African descent of privileges which are essential to freemen. A law that does not allow a colored person to go from one county to another, and one that does not allow him to hold property, to teach, to preach, are certainly laws in violation of the rights of a freeman. The purpose of this bill is to destroy all these discriminations."[21]

Congress passed both bills, but Johnson on March 27 vetoed them. He claimed Congress did not have the power to enforce the bills because of states' rights, a theory that says the federal government has only limited power to tell states how to treat their citizens. He called the measures a "stride toward centralization of all legislative powers in the national Government" and even claimed they amounted to "reverse discrimination [because] the distinction of race and color is by the bill made to operate in favor of the colored and against the white race."[22]

The Senate failed to override Johnson's veto of the bureau bill by a single vote. The bureau measure, however, won approval when it was reintroduced in July. Stunningly, on April 9, 1866, both houses of Congress mustered the two-thirds majority necessary to override Johnson's veto of the Civil Rights Bill. It was the first time an important piece of legislation became law after

President Andrew Johnson unsuccessfully traveled to major cities to gain support for Lincoln's Reconstruction plan.

a president had vetoed it. The political battle between the legislative and executive branches of government was now in full swing.

Radical Republicans Control Reconstruction

The Reconstruction conflict between the president and Congress became the focus of the 1866 congressional elections. The president tried to drum up support for his plan with speeches in major cities like New York, Philadelphia, and Chicago. When Johnson spoke, he was often rudely heckled by people who favored the Radical plan. So many people voted Republican that the party was able to increase its majority in the House and Senate. Their new political power allowed the Republicans to scrap Johnson's Reconstruction efforts and start all over again with their own.

The Fifteenth Amendment gave African Americans the right to vote.

In a special session of Congress, Radical Republicans on March 2, 1867, passed the First Reconstruction Act. The act declared martial law in ten of eleven Confederate states—Tennessee had been readmitted in July 1866 because it met Radical Republican standards—and carved the former Confederacy into five military districts. Military officers and civilian leaders appointed by Congress would govern them until the states met new guidelines. To be readmitted, states had to create new constitutions in conventions that included blacks and had to create a form of government that guaranteed blacks basic rights such as being able to vote.

The Radical Republicans had become so powerful that they now had a chance to accomplish their underlying goal in Reconstruction, which was to rehabilitate the former Confederate states completely from their racist ways. "The whole fabric of Southern society must be changed,"[23] said Stevens. The Reconstruction Act and many additional laws the Radicals passed provided protection for the freed slaves from whites who had denied them their rights and mistreated them for more than two centuries.

Radical Republicans during Reconstruction also proposed three constitutional amendments to safeguard African American rights. The states ratified all three amendments. The Thirteenth Amendment in 1865 abolished slavery throughout the United States; the Emancipation Proclamation had only covered Confederate states. The Fourteenth Amendment in 1868 guaranteed citizenship and federal civil rights to all people born or naturalized in the United States except Native Americans, who would not be granted citizenship until 1924. The Fifteenth Amendment in 1870 guaranteed blacks the right to vote by saying that right could not be denied by race, color, or previous condition of servitude.

There was little Johnson could do to stop what became known as Congressional Reconstruction, because the Radical Republicans had enough votes to override his vetoes of their bills. The Republicans had so much political might that they tried to remove him from office.

Impeaching a President

Johnson after 1867 no longer posed a threat to Radical Reconstruction. But Republicans hated him for the style of Reconstruction he had tried to impose on the nation. They decided to

What Equality Means

■

Benjamin F. Randolph, a black man from South Carolina, explained in 1868 what he meant when he said that "all men are born free and equal." He said the phrase had nothing to do with the color of a person's skin or any other physical attribute. Said Randolph:

It always seemed strange to me that any intelligent person should question the meaning of the phrase. We know that some men are born tall, some short, some with good sense, some with little sense, some with big and some with little feet. But this phrase was not intended to refer to men in a physiological sense. It refers to the rights of men politically speaking and in that sense I understand and defend it. All men are born with certain inalienable rights which it is their privilege to enjoy.

Quoted in Dorothy Sterling, ed., *The Trouble They Seen: Black People Tell the Story of Reconstruction.* New York: Doubleday, 1976, p. 127.

punish him by impeaching him. Impeachment is a safeguard in the Constitution that allows Congress to remove a president who has committed a crime or done something to hurt the nation.

The first effort to impeach Johnson failed on December 7, 1867, when the House voted 108 to 57 against trying the president, because there was no evidence he had actually done anything wrong. A second effort began February 24, 1868, when Pennsylvania representative John Covode introduced a resolution asking that "Andrew Johnson, President of the United States, be impeached [for] high crimes and misdemeanors in office."[24] The House voted 126 to 47 to try Johnson even though no charges were specified in the impeachment resolution. The second effort was ignited by Johnson's decision to fire Secretary of War Edwin M. Stanton, who had angered him by working with the Radicals. That action violated the tenure law, a law Congress had passed that made it illegal for the president to remove a cabinet member without congressional permission. The eleven impeachment charges the House filed against Johnson were vaguely worded and included the claim that he was guilty of criticizing Congress by using "utterances, declarations, threats, and harangues unbecoming in the Chief Magistrate of the United States."[25] The most serious charges centered on the president's violation of the tenure law.

Under the Constitution, the House has the power to file impeachment charges against a president, and the Senate has the power to try the president. Johnson's trial began on March 5 and lasted until May 26. Three separate votes on various charges were taken; all three times, 35 senators voted "guilty" while 19 voted "not guilty." The Constitution requires a two-thirds majority for conviction in impeachment trials, and the Senate failed to impeach Johnson by just one vote. The impeachment failure did not really matter. Johnson had less than a year left in his term and was powerless to stop Radical Republican legislation.

Powerful Radical Republicans were able to begin impeachment proceedings against President Andrew Johnson. This happened even though Johnson had done nothing wrong, except to try to enforce Lincoln's vision of Reconstruction.

When Johnson removed Stanton, General William T. Sherman had accurately commented that "he attempts to govern after he has lost the means to govern. He is like a General fighting without an army."[26] This analysis aptly summed up how badly Johnson had lost his fight with Radical Republicans.

Death of a Radical

Pennsylvania representative Thaddeus Stevens and many other Radical Republicans fought for their brand of Reconstruction because they hated the inhumane way Southern whites had always

Changing the U.S. Constitution

■

Three amendments were added to the U.S. Constitution during Reconstruction. After Congress passed them, states had to approve them individually to ratify them. Below are the amendments and the dates they were ratified:

13th Amendment (December 6, 1865): Section 1. Neither slavery nor involuntary servitude, except as a punishment for crime whereof the party shall have been duly convicted, shall exist within the United States, or any place subject to their jurisdiction.

14th Amendment (July 9, 1868): Section 1. All persons born or naturalized in the United States, and subject to the jurisdiction thereof, are citizens of the United States and of the State wherein they reside. No State shall make or enforce any law which shall abridge the privileges or immunities of citizens of the United States; nor shall any State deprive any person of life, liberty, or property, without due process of law; nor deny to any person within its jurisdiction the equal protection of the laws.

15th Amendment (February 3, 1870): Section 1. The right of citizens of the United States to vote shall not be denied or abridged by the United States or by any State on account of race, color, or previous condition of servitude.

Quoted in National Archives Experience, "Constitution of the United States." www.archives.gov/national-archives-experience/charters/constitution.html.

treated blacks. Stevens had worked for years before the war to overturn slavery; afterward, he wanted blacks to have racial equality. The seventy-six-year-old Stevens was on the verge of realizing that dream when he died on August 11, 1868. Stevens believed in racial equality so much that he chose to be buried in a Lancaster, Pennsylvania, cemetery that was restricted to blacks. He wrote the following inscription for his tombstone: "I repose in this quiet and secluded spot, not from any natural preference for solitude, but finding other cemeteries limited as to race, by charter rules [they did not allow black burials], I have chosen this that I might illustrate in my death the principles which I advocated through a long life, equality of man before his Creator."[27]

Chapter Two

From Slavery to Freedom

Ten days before his death in 1865, President Abraham Lincoln went to Richmond, Virginia. Union soldiers had captured the Confederate capital just two days before the president's visit. As Lincoln walked through the city, slaves who had been freed by the Union army gathered around the man they believed most responsible for giving them their liberty. Many of them joyfully screamed, "Glory, Hallelujah!" and one woman shouted "I know I am free for I have seen Father Abraham."[28] When a black man got down on his knees to thank Lincoln, the president told him: "Don't kneel to me. That is not right. You must kneel to God only, and thank Him for the liberty you will enjoy hereafter."[29]

Those former slaves were among many African Americans who were freed from bondage before the Civil War ended on April 9, 1865. The emancipation of Southern slaves occurred gradually as the North, bit by bit, took control of the eleven rebel states. In fact, former slaves who were now Union army soldiers had helped liberate Richmond and were patrolling its streets when Lincoln arrived. But whenever or however emancipation came, it was a joyous occasion for men, women, and children who were no longer slaves.

The Joy of Freedom

The feeling of freedom was the sweetest emotion that twenty-year-old Henry Holloway of Georgia had ever experienced. "I felt like a bird out of a cage. Amen. Amen. Amen. I could hardly ask to feel any better than I did that day,"[30] Holloway said of the day his life as a slave ended in 1865. Six weeks later, Holloway's happiness grew even greater when his son was born free and not a slave. Holloway

Abraham Lincoln rides through Richmond, Virginia, to the cheers of the city's newly-freed black citizens.

had been sold three different times before he was twenty; he knew that terrible experience would never happen to his son.

Many African Americans celebrated wildly when they were freed. Patsy Moore explains the joyous way fellow Mississippi blacks reacted when they realized they were no longer slaves: "When freedom come, folks left home, out in the streets, crying, praying, singing, shouting, yelling and knocking down everything."[31] One reason their emotions were so strong is that the freedom they had waited for so long arrived so suddenly. Said Felix Haywood, a Texas slave: "The end of the war [and freedom], it comes just like that—like you snap your fingers. Hallelujah broke out."[32]

The desire of some slaves for freedom was so great that they had not been content to wait for the Union army to arrive. Even though they would be killed if they were caught, slaves used the chaos of war to escape to areas the Union army already held. One of the

How Slavery Separated Families

■

Julia Brown was a slave in Commerce, Georgia, until the Civil War ended when she was thirteen years old. She and her mother were owned by the same person but not her father, whom she rarely saw. Brown had five brothers and sisters, but they were sold when she was young. Brown explains how slave families were broken apart:

> There was six of us chillens [but] we didn't stay together long, as we was give out to different people. . . . Oh! it was pitiful to see chillen taken from their mothers' breasts, mothers sold, husbands sold from wives. My uncle was married, but he was owned by one master and his wife was owned by another. He was allowed to visit his wife on Wednesday and Saturday, that's the onliest time he could get off. He went [one] Wednesday and when he went back on Saturday his wife had been bought by the speculator [slave trader] and he never did know where she was.

Quoted in Norman R. Yetman, ed., *Voices from Slavery*. New York: Holt, Rinehart and Winston, 1970, p. 47.

A slave, Robert Smalls, captured this Confederate gunboat, the *Planter*, and used it to escape to the North.

most daring dashes to freedom was made by Robert Smalls, a slave who was the pilot of the *Planter*, a Confederate gunboat. Smalls in May 1862 disguised himself as the ship's captain and sneaked his family onboard. He and other slaves sailed the boat out of the harbor in Charleston, South Carolina, and surrendered to Union ships blockading the port. Said Smalls, "I thought the *Planter* might be of some use to Uncle Abe."[33] He joined the Union navy and, like many other former slaves, helped defeat the Confederacy to make sure his freedom could never be taken away from him again.

Fighting for Their Freedom

The Union refused to allow blacks to become soldiers when the Civil War began, even though thousands had volunteered. One of them was Virginia slave Harry Jarvis, who early in the war escaped to Fortress Monroe and told General Benjamin F. Butler he wanted to fight the Confederates. Jarvis said the general turned him down: "I went to him and asked him to enlist, but he said *it wasn't a black man's war*. I told him it *would* be a black man's war before they got through."[34] Two years later, however, Jarvis did join the Union army.

When the fighting began, however, the Union did begin hiring blacks to work as cooks, laborers, and laundresses in army camps. The number of blacks in army camps swelled to the thousands in the first two years of the war. Slaves escaped from their masters and traveled to Union-controlled areas so they would be free or were emancipated by Union victories. The Union army called the blacks "contrabands." The name was short for "contra-

After the Emancipation Proclamation was issued, blacks were allowed to enlist in the Union army.

African American Medal of Honor Winners in the Civil War

■

Anderson, Aaron	U.S. Navy Landsman
Anderson, Bruce	U.S. Army Private
Barnes, William Henry	U.S. Army Private
Beaty, Powhatan	U.S. Army First Sergeant
Blake, Robert	U.S. Navy Contraband
Bronson, James H.	U.S. Army First Sergeant
Brown, William H.	U.S. Navy Landsman
Brown, Wilson	U.S. Navy Landsman
Carney, William Harvey	U.S. Army Sergeant
Dorsey, Decatur	U.S. Army First Lieutenant & Adjutant
Fleetwood, Christian A.	U.S. Army Sergeant Major
Gardiner, James	U.S. Army Private
Harris, James H.	U.S. Army Private
Hawkins, Thomas R.	U.S. Army Sergeant Major
Hilton, Alfred B.	U.S. Army Sergeant
Holland, Milton Murray	U.S. Army Sergeant Major
James, Miles	U.S. Army First Corporal
Kelly, Alexander	U.S. Army Sergeant
Lawson, John H.	U.S. Navy Landsman
Mifflin, James	U.S. Navy Engineer's Cook
Pease, Joachim	U.S. Navy Seaman
Pinn, Robert A.	U.S. Army First Sergeant
Ratcliff, Edward	U.S. Army First Sergeant
Smith, Andrew Jackson	U.S. Army Corporal
Veal, Charles	U.S. Army Private

Source: The Official Site of the Medal of Honor: African American Civil War: http://click.medalof honor.com/AfricanAmericanCivilWar.htm.

bands of war," meaning something an army has won by fighting. The army employed many of the former slaves and cared for the others, including women and children.

Many blacks went from being contrabands to soldiers in 1863 after Lincoln issued the Emancipation Proclamation. His order authorized the army to enlist blacks because he believed they

Cavalry soldiers commanded by General Nathan Bedford Forrest massacre black Union soldiers at Fort Pillow, Tennessee.

should have a chance to fight for their freedom. More than 180,000 African Americans served in the army and 24,000 in the navy. They fought valiantly. One-third of black soldiers or sailors died in battle or of wounds or disease, and fifteen received the Congressional Medal of Honor, the nation's highest award for courage in combat. Sergeant William H. Carney of the famed Fifty-fourth Massachusetts Volunteer Colored Infantry was the first African American recipient of the prestigious medal. In July 1863 he helped capture Fort Wagner on Morris Island, South Carolina. Although wounded and bleeding heavily, Carney placed the U.S. flag atop the captured Confederate fort. "Boys, the old flag never touched the ground,"[35] Carney told soldiers who then carried him to the rear to receive medical treatment.

It was difficult and dangerous to be a black soldier. Until they began proving themselves in battle, African Americans had trouble being accepted by white soldiers, many of whom were racist. The Confederates also cruelly treated black soldiers whom they captured, and sometimes they even sold them back into slavery. The worst incident of brutality against black soldiers occurred in Tennessee on April 12, 1864, when Confederate forces captured the Union's Fort Pillow. Two hundred of 262 black soldiers died in that battle, but many of them were murdered after surrendering. Ransome Anderson of the United States Colored Heavy Artillery was one of the few black survivors. He explained what happened: "Most all the men that were killed on our side were killed after the fight was over. They [Confederates] called them out and shot them down."[36] The Confederates were led by General Nathan Bedford Forrest, who after the war helped found the Ku Klux Klan.

Blacks did not mind the dangers and hardships they faced, because being a soldier gave them a sense of pride that helped them shed the stigma of having been slaves. It also eased their transition from slavery to freedom, a passage that was often difficult for former slaves.

Adjusting to Freedom

Whites who tried to justify slavery had often argued that blacks were better off as slaves because they were not intelligent or disciplined enough to care for themselves. Such racist beliefs were false. Former slaves, however, did encounter many challenges in adjusting to their new status because life as a free person was so different from being a slave.

The problems blacks faced after emancipation included such a seemingly minor issue as their names. One way in which slave owners had tried to deny African Americans their humanity and make them feel like property was to give them only first names. When they were freed, many blacks needed a last name. Some blacks adopted the names of their former owners or the communities in which they lived. Other blacks celebrated their new status by calling themselves Freeman or Liberty or took the names of famous people like presidents Washington, Jefferson, and Lincoln.

Another reason slave owners did not give slaves last names is that they are family names. They did not want blacks to have family ties because they feared such bonds would make their slaves revolt if they tried to sell a member of their family. Many slaves, however, did marry and form family units even though slave owners opposed it and Southern law did not recognize such marriages. Slave sales broke up many families, and by 1858 it was estimated than 18 percent of slave children had little or no contact with their parents.

When slaves were freed, many began searching for those missing relatives. They traveled to towns or plantations to which members of their families had been sold. They also placed notices in black newspapers seeking information about them. Many African Americans searched for their fathers, mothers, siblings, or children for years but never found them. Henry Johnson was one of the lucky ones. Born in Patrick County, Virginia, Johnson was sold as a small child. He never knew his parents until after the war, when his father tracked him down. Johnson describes the joyous reunion that occurred when his father brought him home: "I never even saw my mother and father until I was in my twenties. When he got me there, I found two sisters and four brothers. They was all so glad to see me they shouted and cried

Henry Adams Knew He Was Free

Some whites at the end of the Civil War tried to convince their freed slaves that they would be better off staying and working for them. But Henry Adams, a twenty-two-year-old slave on a Louisiana plantation, was not convinced of that argument. Like many former slaves, he left his old plantation to test his new independence. Adams explains how his former owner tried to make him stay:

> The white men read a paper to all of us colored people telling us that we were free and could go where we pleased and work for who we pleased. The man I belonged to told me it was best to stay with him. He said, "The bad white men was mad with the Negroes because they were free and they would kill you all for fun." He said, stay where we are living and we could get protection from our old masters. I told him I thought that every man, when he was free, could have his rights and protect themselves.

Quoted in Dorothy Sterling, ed., *The Trouble They Seen: Black People Tell the Story of Reconstruction.* New York: Doubleday, 1976, p. 6.

This illustration depicts the great numbers of African Americans who left their homes in search of a better life in the North.

and carried on so I was so scared I tried to run away, 'cause I didn't know nothin' about none of them. [When] my folks stopped rejoicin', my mother killed and cooked two chickens for me."[37]

Unlike Johnson's family, many freed slaves no longer had homes. As slaves, they had lived in quarters provided by their owners. Some freed blacks continued working for their former owners because they had no place to go, but many decided to find a new place to live. Patience Johnson had been a slave on a large South Carolina plantation. After Johnson was freed, she refused an offer to stay and work for wages. Johnson told the woman who had owned her, "No, Miss, I must go, if I stay here

I'll never know I am free."[38] Tens of thousands of freed slaves left their former homes to find better lives for themselves. Robert Falls was one of them. Years later Falls said, "I remember so well how the roads was full of folks walking and walking along." And even though Falls and many other blacks were not quite sure where they were going or what they would do when they got there, he was buoyed by one bright thought: "And then I begins to think and to know I never had to be a slave no more."[39]

Most blacks had toiled on plantations in rural areas. Many of them traveled to larger communities because they thought there would be more jobs there. But without money to buy food or shelter, few job skills, and little education, many blacks had trouble surviving in the months after they were freed. Felix Hayward was raised a slave in Texas. Hayward admitted that it did not take long for many blacks to realize that the reality of being free was much different from their dreams of freedom: "We knowed freedom was on us, but we didn't know what was to come with it. We thought we was going to get rich like the white folks. We thought we was going to get richer than the white folks, 'cause we were stronger and knowed how to work. [But] it didn't turn out that way. We soon found out that freedom could make folks proud but it didn't make 'em rich."[40]

The federal government, however, had realized the freed slaves would need help adjusting to freedom. The agency that offered help was known as the Freedmen's Bureau.

Helping Former Slaves

Congress on March 3, 1865, passed a bill that created the Bureau of Refugees, Freedmen and Abandoned Lands. The agency, which became popularly known as the Freedmen's Bureau, gave freed slaves food, clothing, and medical care and helped them find missing family members. The most pressing initial problem was feeding the former slaves, especially because food was scarce in the war-ravaged South. The bureau from 1865 to 1867 gave blacks 15.5 million rations—a military term for a meal. The bureau also served nearly 6 million rations to poor whites.

The bureau also helped former slaves find new jobs. It even aided them in negotiating pay and other benefits, something they had never done before. After the war ended, Robert Glenn's owner took him to the Freedmen's Bureau in Dickenson, Kentucky. Glenn wanted to continue working for the man, and the bureau helped them agree on a one-year contract in which his former owner would pay Glenn seventy-five dollars in wages plus room and board. The bureau also made sure that black workers like him were not mistreated. Said Glenn, "The [bureau agent] told me to let him know if I was not paid as agreed."[41] Glenn stayed with his former owner for one year. He then left to work for a doctor who paid him more.

Many former slaves had trouble getting jobs because they had few skills and little or no education. Most black males had worked as field hands on farms and cotton plantations; most women had worked inside the homes of Southerners doing a variety of

Newly freed blacks are told about their new freedoms at the Freedmen's Bureau in Memphis, Tennessee. The Bureau also gave food, clothing, and shelter to blacks.

domestic chores. Few freed slaves knew how to read or write. Slave owners had routinely kept blacks from becoming educated because they feared that education would ignite a desire in slaves to be free. They believed it was so important to keep their slaves ignorant that they severely punished or killed those who tried to learn to read and write.

One of the most important things the bureau did was to begin educating freed slaves. In the six years the bureau was in operation, it set up more than one thousand schools throughout the South. Some schools held sessions during the day and at night so that people who worked during the day could still attend school. The bureau also built permanent schools for blacks and helped establish the first black universities such as Alcorn, Howard, Southern, and Fisk.

Hundreds of thousands of blacks flocked to the schools, some of which were organized and funded with the help of Northern church and humanitarian groups. Blacks hungered for education because they realized it would help them in their new lives.

"A Whole Race" Goes to School

Tens of thousands of adults went to school because they had been denied that opportunity as slaves. J.W. Alvord, a Freedmen's Bureau agent in North Carolina, noted in 1866 that several generations of one family had learned to read. "A child six years old, her mother, grandmother and great-grandmother, the latter over 75 years of age [began] their alphabet together and each one can [now] read fluently."[42] Another agent in Tennessee explained how highly former slaves valued a chance to become educated: "The colored people are far more zealous in the cause of education than the whites. They will starve themselves, and go without [new] clothes, in order to send their children to school."[43]

One of the former slaves who thirsted for knowledge was Booker T. Washington. Born into slavery in Virginia on April 5, 1856, Washington could neither read nor write when the Civil War ended. After being freed, Washington worked at menial jobs as a laborer for several years before he began attending a Virginia school for blacks that eventually became Hampton University.

Washington became a teacher himself, and in 1881 he was named to head a new school in Alabama which today is known as Tuskegee University. Washington for several decades was one of the nation's most prominent and powerful African American leaders. He dedicated himself to educating blacks and helping them achieve equality with whites. Washington always said that he owed his success to being educated, and he once fondly recalled how hungry Southern blacks were to learn after they were freed: "It was a whole race trying to go to school. Few were too young, and none too old, to make the attempt to learn. As fast as any kind of teachers could be secured, not only were day-schools filled but night-schools as well."[44]

Many other former slaves became teachers. Isabella Gibbins began teaching in Charlottesville, Virginia, after she learned to read and write herself. She had forty-one students in her first class when she began teaching on October 15, 1866. The parents

A Teacher Praises Black Students

Charlotte Forten was born in Philadelphia. After the Union captured South Carolina, Forten in 1862 became the first African American who went south to teach former slaves. Forten taught students for two years on St. Helena Island. In an article in the March 1864 edition of *Atlantic Monthly* magazine, Forten commented on how much her students loved learning:

> I never before saw children so eager to learn, although I had had several years experience in New-England schools. Coming to school is a constant delight and recreation to them. They come here as other children go to play. The older ones, during the summer, work in the fields from early morning until eleven or twelve o-clock, and then come to school, after their hard toil in the hot sun, as bright and as anxious to learn as ever. . . . Many of the grown people are desirous of learning to read. It is wonderful how a people who have been so long crushed to the earth can have so great a desire for knowledge, and such a capacity for attaining it.

Quoted in William Loren Katz, *Eyewitness: The Negro in American History*. New York: Pittman, 1971, p. 251.

African Americans attend a school during Reconstruction. More than one thousand schools were set up to educate freed blacks.

of the students all decided to enroll them in school after an introductory meeting in which Gibbins read compositions written by her son, John, and other former slaves. Gibbins said members of the audience were impressed that other blacks could read and write so well: "I think it did great good. They seemed as though their eyes had just been opened to see what education would do for them."[45] In addition to black educators like Gibbins and Washington, hundreds of Northern whites came south to help teach freed slaves.

"What Is Freedom?"

The reason white teachers wanted to help the blacks is that they knew that merely releasing African Americans from slavery would not insure that they could have a decent life. Republican representative James A. Garfield in 1865 concisely expressed that idea when he asked "What is freedom? Is it the bare privilege of not being chained? If this is all, then freedom is a bitter mockery, a cruel delusion."[46] During Reconstruction, the federal government tried to make sure blacks could gain the true freedom that Garfield talked about.

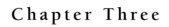

Fighting for Equality with Whites

James K. Green was born in 1823 on one of the largest plantations in Hale County, Alabama. His emancipation at the end of the Civil War opened up a new life for him that was far different from the one he had led as a slave. During Reconstruction, Green helped write Alabama's new state constitution and served eight years in the Alabama legislature. Years later, Green commented on how being freed had completely changed his life: "I was entirely ignorant; I knew nothing more than to obey my masters; and there was thousands of us in the same attitude. But the tocsin [ringing bell sound] of freedom sounded and knocked at the door and we walked out like free men and shouldered the responsibilities."[47]

Green and other African Americans who served in Southern state legislatures and Congress during Reconstruction reached positions of power and political influence that few people had ever believed possible for former slaves. They used their new status to try to achieve true equality with Southern whites. Their battle for acceptance was difficult, however, because the

African American members of the South Carolina legislature participate in the passage of an appropriations bill.

racism that had been the rationale for slavery was still strong in the South.

Free but Not Equal

The only major concession former Confederate states had to make when President Andrew Johnson began readmitting them to the Union was to approve the Thirteenth Amendment, which abolished slavery. The states then drafted constitutions that still denied blacks basic rights such as being able to vote and further curtailed their liberty by passing so-called black codes. This unfair treatment of African Americans was coupled with brutal racial violence; thousands of freed slaves endured beatings, whippings, and murder.

The twin assaults on freed slaves led Radical Republicans to impose their own Reconstruction plan to make sure blacks would be treated equally with whites. Before the states could be readmitted, Congress forced them to draft new constitutions that guaranteed blacks their rights as U.S. citizens. One way Congress insured that would happen was to allow blacks to vote for delegates to the conventions that drafted constitutions, something that they had been denied when Southern states first drafted new constitutions under Presidential Reconstruction. The African Americans elected to the conventions helped write constitutions that guaranteed them the rights that whites had.

Congress also strengthened those civil rights by passing the Fourteenth Amendment to the U.S. Constitution. The Fourteenth Amendment guarantees blacks citizenship and equal rights. Pennsylvania representative Thaddeus Stevens said the measure was so necessary to protect the freed slaves from racist treatment that "I can hardly believe that any person can be found who will not admit that [it] is just."[48]

The Fourteenth Amendment was ratified by the states on July 9, 1868. Even before it became part of the U.S. Constitution, blacks and whites were already working together to establish such rights in the former Confederacy.

Blacks and Whites Work Together

In 1867 and 1868, former slaves sat down with former slave owners and other whites in every Southern state to draft new constitutions. Delegates to the constitutional conventions were chosen by nearly 1.4 million eligible voters in the ten states that needed to be reconstructed; Tennessee was the lone Confederate state that had already been readmitted. The pool of eligible voters included 703,000 blacks and 627,000 whites. There would have been more white voters, but about 150,000 former Confederate soldiers and government officials were prohibited from voting because of their wartime actions.

Even though there were more black than white voters in South Carolina, Florida, Mississippi, Alabama, and Louisiana, more white delegates were elected in every state except South Carolina.

In Mississippi, for example, whites outnumbered blacks 84 to 16. Thus blacks usually had to depend on whites to write constitutions that treated them equally. One of those whites was James L. Alcorn, a Mississippi plantation owner who before the war had owned sixty slaves. Even though his two sons had died fighting for the Confederacy, Alcorn aligned himself with blacks to create a better future for his state. He went into the conven-

An illustration depicts the reconstructed constitution of Louisiana, which prominently figures blacks as part of the process. During Reconstruction, blacks helped to rewrite their states' constitutions.

tion saying, "The 'old master' [slave owner], gentlemen, has passed from fact to poetry. I will sit in council with the Negro, vote with him, and join him [in agreeing] on a platform [of ideas] acceptable to him as well as to the whites."[49] Alcorn in 1869 would be elected governor of Mississippi.

South Carolina was the only state convention that had a black majority. Out of 131 delegates, 76 were black, two-thirds of them freed slaves including Joseph Rainey. A former slave who escaped to freedom during the Civil War, Rainey in 1868 became the first African American elected to the U.S. House of Representatives. Years after the convention, Rainey proudly declared that blacks had treated whites fairly in drafting the historic document: "Our convention which met in 1868, and in which Negroes were in a large majority adopted a liberal constitution, securing alike equal rights to all citizens, white and black, male and female, as far as possible. Mark you we did not discriminate, although we had a majority."[50]

Joseph Rainey was the first black elected to the House of Representatives.

The South Carolina constitution approved universal suffrage for men of any race (women were still not allowed to vote) and ended many types of discrimination, such as prohibiting blacks from attending public school. The constitution included other progressive provisions such as outlawing dueling, eliminating the requirement of owning property to hold office, and ending the practice of imprisoning people who could not pay their debts.

Other Southern states incorporated similar ideals in their new constitutions as a new era of African American equality in the South seemed to open. The reality of the situation, however, was that most Southern whites did not want blacks to have those rights.

Racist Whites Were Unhappy

After the South Carolina Constitution had been written, many whites claimed it did not represent their views because it gave blacks equality. They also derided the document as "the work of sixty-odd negroes, many of them ignorant and depraved, together with fifty white men, outcasts of Northern society, and southern renegades, betrayers of their race and country."[51] In North Carolina, where there were only 15 blacks out of 133 delegates, whites also criticized their state's new constitution and crudely characterized the delegates who drafted it as "baboons, monkeys, mules, Tourgee [white Northerners], and other jackasses.[52]

In the first two years after the Civil War ended, Carl Schurz investigated conditions in Southern states for President Johnson. Schurz, a German immigrant and former Union officer, discovered that most Southerners still believed blacks were inferior and refused to accept them as their equals. Schurz wrote: "Wherever I go—the street, the shop, the house, the hotel, or the steamboat—I hear the people talk in such a way as to indicate that they're yet unable to conceive of the Negro as possessing any rights at all. Whites will cheat a Negro without feeling a single twinge of honor. To kill a Negro, they do not deem murder."[53]

The new constitutions did not reflect the racism that predominated among whites in much of the South, because many people with such beliefs were not eligible to vote to elect convention delegates. Thousands of former Confederate officials and soldiers in each state were not allowed to vote to elect delegates. And the federal government for the first time allowed blacks to vote, something many Southern whites opposed. The result was that the delegations included African Americans, transplanted Northerners (most of them former Union soldiers), and Southerners who believed blacks should have a chance at equality.

For the same reason, disgruntled whites could not stop approval of the constitutions even though they disagreed with the high ideals they contained. They also could not stop African

He Would Accept Only Equality

One of the delegates to the South Carolina constitutional convention was Francis L. Cardozo. Born free in Charleston, South Carolina, he was educated at the University of Glasgow in Scotland. Cardozo proposed a clause to the constitution that said no citizen could be deprived of rights because of race or color. When some whites objected, this is how he defended it:

> As colored men we have been cheated out of our rights for two centuries and now that we have the opportunity I want to fix them in the Constitution in such a way that no lawyer, however cunning, can possibly misinterpret the meaning. Nearly all of the white inhabitants of the State are ready at any moment to deprive us of these rights and not a loophole should be left that would permit them to do it. By all means insert the words "without distinction of race or color" wherever necessary to give force and clearness to our laws.

Quoted in Dorothy Sterling, ed., *The Trouble They Seen: Black People Tell the Story of Reconstruction.* New York: Doubleday, 1976, p. 128.

Francis L. Cardozo argued that the Constitution should explicitly state that rights should be guaranteed to blacks.

Americans from becoming part of the governments that controlled their lives.

Blacks Govern the South

During Reconstruction about two thousand blacks held office in Southern states. They served in every conceivable post, from justice of the peace to governor as well as U.S. senator. The first and only black Reconstruction governor was Pinckney Benton Stewart Pinchback. On December 9, 1872, this son of a white plantation owner and freed slave became Louisiana's governor after Governor Henry C. Warmoth was impeached. Pinchback, who had been lieutenant governor, served for thirty-five days until a white governor was elected on January 13, 1873. There would not be another black Southern governor until Douglas Wilder was elected in Virginia in 1990.

Blanche Kelso Bruce was one of sixteen African Americans to serve in Congress during Reconstruction.

The black local, state, and national officials and legislators included former slaves, blacks who had been free before the war, and Northern blacks who had moved south. Most of the blacks had some education, even if it was only a short period of schooling after emancipation, and some had college degrees. Georgia lawmaker Abram Colby, however, was illiterate. Colby solved that problem by having his son, who could read and write, stay by his side to help him.

Black officials and legislators generally got high marks for the way they conducted themselves, mainly because the programs they helped propose and pass benefited all state residents. As Speaker of the House in Mississippi, former slave John R. Lynch helped enact programs that repaired war damage, built new schools and hospitals, and helped strengthen transportation by expanding state railroads. In 1872 James Pike, a newspaper reporter for the *New York Times*, wrote the following comment about black legislators: "Seven years ago these men were raising corn and cotton under the whip of an overseer. Today they are raising points of order and questions of privilege [in legislative debates]. They can raise one as well as the other. [Their new political power] means escape and defense from old oppressors. It means liberty. It means the destruction of prison walls only too real to them."[54]

Sixteen African Americans served in Congress during Reconstruction. About half of the black congressmen were former slaves, including Blanche Kelso Bruce, one of two U.S. senators from Mississippi. Blacks generally drew praise from congressmen they worked with, including James G. Blaine, a U.S. senator from Maine and the Republican Party presidential candidate in 1884. Blaine once said: "The colored men who took seats in both the Senate and the House did not appear ignorant or helpless. They were as a rule studious, earnest, ambitious men whose public conduct would be honorable to any race."[55]

Black lawmakers knew that they and their fellow African Americans faced a difficult task in winning acceptance from whites. When Oscar J. Dunn was sworn in as Louisiana's first black lieutenant governor on November 24, 1868, he tried to quiet the fears of whites by saying he and other blacks had just one goal. "We simply ask," he said, "an equal opportunity of supporting our

A former slave couple work outside their cabin in Virginia. Few blacks were able to own their land.

government's failure to give blacks land after the war was a crushing blow that left a freed slave "on his knees."[69] Blacks who wanted to farm, however, soon found a way to do it in a new style of agriculture called sharecropping.

Working for Whites Again

Sharecropping developed out of the need white landowners had for workers and the desire blacks had to farm individual plots of land. Whites provided blacks with land, housing, seed, fertilizer, tools, and food in return for half to two-thirds of the crop the blacks raised.

This new arrangement was both good and bad for blacks. Some sharecroppers did well and saved enough money to buy

Let Women Vote, Too!

◼

Sojourner Truth was born a slave in the state of New York about 1797. She escaped from slavery in 1826 and became one of the most powerful spokespersons calling for abolition of slavery. Truth was also an early advocate of women's rights. In a speech in 1867, Truth said women deserved rights as well as the freed slaves did:

> There is a great stir about colored men getting their rights, but not a word about the colored women; and if colored men get their rights, and not colored women theirs, you see, the colored men will be masters over the colored women, and it will be just as bad as it was before. [I] want women to have their rights. I am above eighty years old; it is about time for me to be going. I am glad to see that men are getting their rights, but I want women to get theirs.

Quoted in Herb Boyd, ed., *Autobiography of a People: Three Centuries of African American History Told by Those Who Lived It*. New York: Doubleday, 2000, p. 144.

Sojourner Truth fought both to free blacks and for equal rights for women.

their own land; by 1910 blacks owned almost one-third of the land they farmed. Mingo White, a freed Alabama slave, was one of the lucky ones. White explains his success: "Us [his family] made a sharecrop with Mr. John Rawlins. He furnished us with rations and a place to stay. Us'd sell our cotton and corn and pay Mr. John Rawlins for feedin' us. We kept movin' and makin' sharecrops till us saved up 'nough money to [get] us a place and make a crop for ourselves."[61]

But many blacks fell into debt to white landowners and were forced to continue working for the same person indefinitely. One Texas sharecropper noted angrily, "We make as much cotton and sugar as when we were slaves, and it does us as little good now as it did then."[62] Over time, many people came to see sharecropping as an economic form of slavery.

"We Are Not Prepared"

Whether it was owning their own farms or voting and taking part in governing themselves, all blacks wanted was the opportunity to prove they could do it. Beverly Nash was an illiterate former slave and hotel waiter who was elected a delegate to the South Carolina constitutional convention. Even Nash had concerns about the ability of former slaves like himself to vote and write constitutions: "I believe, my friends and fellow citizens, we are not prepared for this suffrage." However, Nash believed that with time blacks could master their new responsibilities as citizens. Said Nash: "But we can learn. Give a man tools and let him commence to use them, and in time he will learn a trade. So it is with voting. We may not understand it at the start, but in time we shall learn to do our duty."[63]

Nash and other African Americans just wanted the chance to prove themselves. During Reconstruction, they got that opportunity.

Chapter Four

Southern Whites Oppose Reconstruction

The end of the Civil War marked the beginning of a wave of brutality and oppression against African Americans in the defeated Confederate states. The Union had abolished slavery by winning the divisive conflict, but it could not make Southern whites accept freed slaves as their equals. Because of that, many whites turned to violence in a savage attempt to intimidate freed slaves into being as submissive as they had been when they were still slaves.

Either singly or in groups, whites beat, whipped, and murdered thousands of blacks for the slightest offense, such as a black not saying "Sir" to a white man. In a story in the *New York Herald* newspaper, a reporter explained that the thousands of violent incidents in the first few months after the war all had a deadly purpose: "It is needless to say that their attention [that of Southern whites] is largely directed to maintaining quiet and submission among the blacks. The shooting or stringing up [hanging] of some obstreperous 'nigger' by the 'regulators' is so common an occurrence as to excite little remark."[64]

Excuses for White Violence

───────────■───────────

The violence whites committed against blacks during the Reconstruction era was rooted in racism. Nearly anything that annoyed a white person could trigger attacks on blacks. Historian Eric Foner gives some of the reasons listed in Freedmen's Bureau reports for assaults and murders of black people:

> An Alabama overseer shot a black worker who "gave him sarse [disrespect]"; a white South Carolina minister "drew his pistol and shot [a freedman] thru the heart" after he objected to the expulsion of another black man from church services. [Foner listed] the "reasons" for some of the 1,000 murders of blacks by whites between 1865 and 1868: One victim "did not remove his hat"; another "wouldn't give up his whisky flask"; a white man "wanted to thin out the niggers a little"; another wanted "to see a nigger kick." Gender offered no protection to black women—one was beaten by her employer for "using insolent language," another for refusing to "call him master," a third "for crying because he whipped my mother."

Eric Foner, *Reconstruction: America's Unfinished Revolution, 1863–1877*. New York: Harper and Row, 1989, p. 120.

"Regulator" was one of several nicknames applied to whites who terrorized blacks. Whatever they were called, they were trying to show blacks that whites were still superior to them even though slavery had been abolished.

Trying to Reenslave Blacks

During slavery, slave owners had often punished or mistreated their slaves. They had rarely killed them, however, because the slaves earned money for their owners by the work they did. This changed when slavery ended. No longer valuable as possessions, whites no longer hesitated to maim or kill black men and women.

Walter White is an African American historian and twentieth-century civil rights crusader. White claims the epidemic of postwar violence against blacks had only one purpose: "The vast majority of the whites of the late Confederacy—even of those who had owned no slaves—were united in a single cause—to re-enslave the negro as far as was humanly possible."[65]

The new form of slavery White wrote about did not include actual ownership of blacks. Instead, it was an attempt to keep African Americans in an inferior position to whites economically, politically, and socially. This effort grew out of the need to find a new racial hierarchy in the South between whites and blacks. Historian James Elbert Cutler explains the situation whites faced: "The relationship of master and slave had been destroyed and no new relationship had yet been firmly established in its place. The emancipation of the slaves and Reconstruction policy had carried out a changed relationship between the two races and made black domination a possibility in the eyes of southerners, who thought it such an evil thing that it justified any means to stop it."[66]

Whites were willing to use force to make blacks accept a new social order in which they once again dominated blacks. Much of this violence erupted in encounters between members of the two races as they went about their daily lives.

"It's Something We Can't Help"

After the Civil War, even as simple a thing as the way blacks and whites greeted each other could spark violence. Reporting on one such incident in Texas, the Freedmen's Bureau said a black man was "killed [shot to death] because he did not take off his hat to Murphy."[67] Tipping your hat was a sign of respect that whites had always expected of blacks when they met in any situation.

Such violent, often deadly incidents were caused by the inability of Southern whites to reject their racist beliefs. In an 1866 book about the postwar South, author J.T. Trowbridge quoted a man who told him Southerners had found it impossible to change their attitudes about blacks: "We can't feel towards them as you [a Northerner] do; I suppose we ought to, but it isn't possible for us. They've always been our owned servants, and we've been used to having them mind us without a word of objection, and we can't bear anything else from them now. If that's wrong, we're to be pitied sooner than blamed, for it's something we can't help."[68]

This inability to see blacks as human beings instead of property was strongest in former slave owners. A Freedmen's Bureau report cites an example that shows how difficult it was for slave owners to realize that the slaves they had once owned were now free people. When an emancipated slave went to a plantation to get his wife, the man who had owned the woman murdered him. The bureau report said: "A great outrage was perpetrated. Fletcher resisted the negro, shot him and afterwards cut off his head."[69]

The former owner had refused to allow the man to take his wife because he still believed he had the right to control his former slave. Attitudes like this resulted in thousands of acts of violence against blacks.

Violence to Control Blacks

In their attempts to make blacks accept an inferior position in society, whites often severely beat them, damaged their homes and businesses, and sometimes killed them. Many of the violent incidents involved whipping, which had been the main punishment for slaves. Whites used whipping as a way to show blacks that whites still controlled them even though slavery had ended. Harriet Hernandes of Spartanburg, South Carolina, testified once before Congress that whites had whipped most of her neighbors: "It is all of them, mighty near. I could not begin to tell all. Ann Bonner and her daughter, Manza Surratt and his wife and whole family, even the least child in the family, they took it out of bed and whipped it. They told them if they did that they would remember it."[70]

The gangs of men often employed rape as a tool of terror. Rhoda Ann Childs was the wife of a former Union soldier. In September 1868, eight men visited her home while her husband was away; they raped her and beat her two daughters. Childs said that one of the men threatened to shoot her with his pistol "as my husband had been in the 'damned Yankee army,' and swore they meant to kill every black they could find that had ever fought against them."[71] Such cruel acts were meant to frighten people like her husband, who had been brave enough to fight Confederate soldiers.

Whites employed this violence to create a climate of fear so that blacks would accept second-class status. Blacks were denied

Many white Southerners used violence to maintain control of blacks.

access to hotels, restaurants, and other public places reserved for whites. When they traveled by train, they had to sit in railroad cars reserved for blacks. These cars were dirtier and more crowded than those whites rode in. Even blacks in important positions were subjected to such unfair treatment. Representative John R. Lynch of Mississippi complained once in a speech in Congress about being forced to ride in the black railroad car even though he had a ticket for the first-class white car. Lynch protested, "I am treated, not as an American citizen, but as a brute."[72]

Most blacks who complained about such treatment were beaten or even killed for daring to demand equality with whites.

Many other blacks were singled out for violence because they tried to better themselves by attending school or were doing well financially. Whites drove Robert Fullerlove off his 400-acre farm (162ha) in Choctaw County, Alabama, because he had become prosperous. In 1872 Fullerlove told a congressional committee investigating such violence, "I never expect to set my foot on it no more."[73] Whites also used the threat of violence to cheat blacks in business dealings. When black sharecroppers divided the crops they had grown with whites who owned the land they farmed, the whites often took more than their fair share. A Freedmen's Bureau agent in Louisiana in 1869 said, "Driving the freedmen from their crop and seizing it themselves when it is grown is a complaint against the planters that comes to us from every quarter."[74]

Individuals perpetrated many violent incidents. However, the majority of beatings and murders were conducted by groups who planned and carried out an organized campaign of terror against blacks.

Organized Terror

Southerners after the Civil War were bitter over their defeat, and during Reconstruction they became angry that the Union was now governing their home states. One Southerner living in Amelia County, Virginia, was so despondent after the war and hated Northerners so much that he killed himself. In a hate-filled suicide note, the man declared, "I hereby claim my unmitigated hatred to Yankee rule—to all political, social and business connections with the Yankees and to the Yankee race."[75] "Yankee" was the derisive Southern term for a Northerner; Southerners also called Northerners who worked as Reconstruction officials "carpetbaggers." Defeated Confederates also hated "scalawags," Southerners who accepted black equality and Reconstruction, but reserved their greatest hatred for blacks, whom they blamed for having caused the war due to the slavery issue.

Confederate soldiers and other Southerners channeled those bitter feelings into violence against the people they hated. They often did this by joining secretive military-style organizations. The groups included the White Camellias, Knights of the Rising Sun, and the Pale Faces, but the most powerful and feared was

The Powerful Ku Klux Klan

In June 1866 a group of former Confederate soldiers started the Ku Klux Klan (KKK). By July 1868 General W.P. Carlin, who headed the Freedmen's Bureau in Tennessee, reported to Washington that the Klan had become a dire menace to blacks:

> Complaints are continually coming in of outrages committed by the Ku Klux Klan. The colored people are leaving their homes, and are fleeing to the towns and large cities for protection. They say that it is impossible for them to work during the day and keep watch during the night, which is necessary for them to do, in order to save their lives. Unless something is done immediately, by the Governor, to protect the colored citizens of the country, the cities will be flooded by poor, helpless creatures, who will have to be supported by the [government]. The Ku Klux organization is so extensive, and so well organized and armed, that it is beyond the power of any one to exert a moral influence over them. Powder and ball is the only thing that will put them down.

Quoted in Philip Dray, *At the Hands of Persons Unknown: The Lynching of Black America*. New York: Random House, 2002, pp. 45–46.

The Ku Klux Klan attacks a black family. The KKK terrorized blacks to make them fear and obey whites.

the Ku Klux Klan (KKK). The Klan was founded in 1866 in Pulaski, Tennessee, and its first leader was Nathan Bedford Forrest, a renowned Confederate cavalry general.

KKK members dressed in white sheets and hoods to conceal their identity. In nighttime raids, Klan members attacked blacks to make them fear and obey whites. W.L. Bost, a freed slave who lived in Newton, North Carolina, said Klan members terrified blacks: "They were terrible dangerous. They ride horses through the town at night and if they find a Negro that tries to get nervy [stand up to whites] or have a little bit for himself, they lash him nearly to death [with whips]."[76]

The Klan's victims included teachers like African American Thomas S. Jones because whites feared blacks becoming educated. In January 1871 Jones wrote the governor of South Carolina to complain that armed whites had threatened him: "Dear sir, it is a plot to drive me out of the country because I am a school teacher."[77] The KKK also attacked white teachers and others who worked for or supported Reconstruction.

The KKK spread to other Southern states and became the chief perpetrator of organized violence against blacks. The Klan became such a problem that Congress in the early 1870s began investigating it. Forrest, who as Grand Wizard was the Klan's top official, told a congressional hearing that the group was created to protect whites from possible violence by freed slaves: "The Negroes were holding night meetings; were going about; were becoming very insolent; and the Southern people all over the State were very much alarmed. There was a great deal of insecurity in the country [rural areas], and I think this [the KKK] was got up to protect the weak."[78]

But J.T. Tims, a freed Alabama slave, had a different view of Klan activities. Said Tims of the whippings and beatings KKK members committed: "They were terrible. They didn't do nothin' but just to keep the [freed] slaves down."[79] And one way whites tried to keep blacks helpless was to prevent them from gaining political power.

Political Violence

Southern whites did not want blacks to vote or hold public office because they could use that power to get equal rights with

Anti-emancipation rioters burn a freedmen's school during a race riot in Memphis, Tennessee, in 1866.

whites. Unable legally or politically to stop blacks from participating in politics, whites turned to violence and intimidation.

Armed whites attacked blacks at political gatherings. In 1868 in Camilla, Georgia, blacks held a parade to gather support for Republican candidates in the coming election. Blacks during Reconstruction voted Republican because the Democratic Party, which before the war had supported slavery, was still the party of those who opposed equal rights for blacks. A group of four hundred whites who supported other candidates attacked the marching blacks, killing more than twenty people and wounding many others. A local black leader said of the attack, "We don't call them

Democrats, we call them southern murderers."[80] The white mob was led by the local sheriff.

Whites resented black officials because of the power they had over them, and they attacked many of them to make them quit their positions. Klan members in Tennessee whipped Andrew J. Flowers when he defeated a white candidate in an election for justice of the peace. "They said that they did not intend any nigger to hold office in the United States,"[81] he said. During Reconstruction, it is believed that whites threatened or physically harmed about 10 percent of black officials and murdered at least thirty-five of them.

Because even elected officials were not safe from such attacks, blacks felt vulnerable. The Reverend Charles Ennis of Georgia in 1869 wrote, "We have no protection at all from the laws of Georgia [and he feared] the whole South would come against us and kill us off, as the Indians have been killed off."[82] Ennis had real cause for such concern. Some acts of violence escalated into race

Whites Beat Abram Colby

■

Georgia state legislator Abram Colby was one of hundreds of black elected officials who were beaten or killed during Reconstruction. Colby describes his beating on October 29, 1869:

> They broke my door open, took me out of bed, took me to the woods and [whipped] me three hours or more and left me for dead. Some are first-class men in our town. One is a lawyer, one a doctor, and some are farmers. They had their pistols and they took me in my night-clothes and carried me from home. [The] worst thing about the whole matter was this. My mother, wife and daughter were in the room when they came. My little daughter begged them not to carry me away. They drew up a gun and actually frightened her to death. She never got over it until she died. That was the part that grieves me the most.

Quoted in Dorothy Sterling, ed., *The Trouble They Seen: Black People Tell the Story of Reconstruction.* New York: Doubleday, 1976, p. 374.

riots in which hundreds of whites indiscriminately attacked any blacks they met.

Race Riots

One of the main causes of race riots during Reconstruction was the fear that whites had over growing black political power. One of the worst occurred July 30, 1866, in New Orleans, Louisiana, when black and white delegates met at the Mechanics' Institute to begin writing a state constitution that would allow blacks to vote. A large group of whites, including former Confederate police officers, firefighters, and former Confederate soldiers, gathered to attack the delegates. Before federal troops could end the violence, 34 black and 3 white delegates had been killed and 146 wounded. Union general Philip Sheridan called the riot "an absolute massacre by the police."[83]

Racism was so widespread in the South that, as in the New Orleans riot, many white public officials took part in the violence. On May 1, 1866, a riot in Memphis, Tennessee, started after white police arrested a black carriage driver for colliding with a white carriage. After black Union veterans forced the police to let the man go, whites retaliated. For three days, white mobs that included many policemen engaged in violence. Forty-six blacks and two whites were killed and hundreds of black homes, churches, and schools were robbed or destroyed.

Another riot that became known as the Colfax Massacre occurred on April 13, 1873, in Colfax, Louisiana. The violence began over which candidates had won contested elections in November 1872. Starting about noon at the local courthouse, more than 300 whites, including KKK members, fought with blacks, including soldiers from Louisiana's almost all-black state militia. The whites then attacked blacks living in the area in a rampage that lasted until police and federal troops from New Orleans quelled the riot the next day. Officials estimated that at least 105 blacks were killed. Historians are not sure, however, how many really died because so many bodies were burned, buried, or hidden.

John G. Lewis, a black teacher and legislator, said the Colfax Massacre taught blacks how defenseless they were against massed groups of whites. Said Lewis: "The organization against [blacks] is too strong."[84] That situation was common for most blacks when faced with white violence. Many blacks, however, faced their tormentors with great bravery.

Black Self-Defense

Abram Colby was a former Georgia slave who was elected to the Georgia state legislature. On the night of October 29, 1869, a group of about thirty men took him from his home and whipped him. The beating came several days after whites had tried to bribe him with five thousand dollars to leave the area because they did not want a black representing them. Colby responded by saying, "I told them that I would not do that if they would give me all the county was worth."[85] Colby refused the bribe even though he realized their next move would almost certainly be to beat or even kill him. The reason the whites were angry at him was that he had recently asked state officials to protect blacks against racist whites.

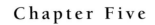

Chapter Five

The End of Reconstruction and Equal Rights

Except for their freedom, the most important thing African Americans gained during Reconstruction was the right to vote. The power to elect public officials who were not racist, especially other blacks, was considered the key to ensuring that they would be treated as equals. That is why Frederick Douglass was ecstatic when the Fifteenth Amendment to the Constitution was ratified. The former slave claimed that "at last, the black man has a future. The black man is free, the black man is a citizen, the black man is enfranchised [able to vote]. Never was revolution more complete."[86]

Douglass believed approval of the amendment on February 3, 1870, had secured that valuable right for blacks forever. Only seven years later, however, Douglass's dream of equality for blacks would end along with Reconstruction. His vision for black equality and Reconstruction would both die when racist whites regained political control in the former Confederate states due to the growing indifference of Northern whites over the fate of the freed slaves.

Whites Battle for Supremacy

Whites who opposed black rights were politically weak when Reconstruction began because about 150,000 former Confederate soldiers and officials were barred from voting. Despite this, some racist whites were elected and used their positions to try to stop blacks from achieving equality. An example of this occurred in September 1868, when white members of the Georgia state legislature had enough votes to refuse to allow black members who had been legally elected to serve as legislators. Georgia, in seeking readmission to the Union, had approved a Constitution that ensured blacks equality with whites, including the right to vote and hold office. The action by the racist white legislators went against the principles set down in Georgia's state constitution.

A U.S. soldier defends a black man against a white Southerner. White Southerners often disregarded laws that gave black citizens rights.

South Carolina Red Shirt

■

The violence whites used to keep blacks from voting was highly organized. In South Carolina during the 1876 election, much of the violence
was done by whites who were collectively called "Red Shirts." Martin W.
Gary, one of the leaders of the effort to elect Wade Hampton governor, issued instructions on how to attack blacks. Gary's orders are chilling in the
casual way in which they suggest beating and killing blacks. This excerpt
from them is from *Black Power U.S.A.: The Human Side of Reconstruction,
1867–1877* by Lerone Bennett Jr.:

> Every Democrat must feel honor bound to control the vote of at
> least one Negro, by intimidation, purchase, keeping him away or
> as each individual may determine, how he may best accomplish it.
> Never threaten a man individually. If he deserves to be threatened,
> the necessities of the time require that he should die. A dead Radi-
> cal is very harmless—a threatened Radical or one driven off by
> threats from the scene of his operation is often very troublesome,
> sometimes dangerous, always vindictive.

Quoted in Lerone Bennett Jr., *Black Power U.S.A.: The Human Side of Reconstruction, 1867–1877.*
Chicago: Johnson, 1967, p. 373.

The federal government punished Georgia by placing it under
military rule and making it begin the Reconstruction process
anew. Many Georgia whites approved the attempt to keep blacks
out of the legislature even though it had failed. The *Jackson Clar-
ion* newspaper called legislators who voted out blacks "a noble
band whose names will long be remembered by their country-
men."[87] Georgia was not readmitted until July 15, 1870.

Southern whites gained new political strength in 1872 when
Congress passed the Amnesty Act. This bill allowed most former
Confederate loyalists to vote again. The Democratic Party had
historically favored white domination, and the newly enfranchised whites began helping Democratic candidates win elections over Republicans. When whites did not have enough votes
to win, they often resorted to violence to stop blacks from voting. After Democrat John McEnery lost the 1872 election for

Louisiana governor, he vowed, "We shall carry the next election if we have to ride saddle-deep in blood to do it."[88]

In the next few years, McEnery and Southerners in other states made that threat a reality with a widespread terror campaign to keep blacks from voting. Whites in Southern states in 1874 began organizing themselves into groups called White Leagues. They beat blacks, burned their homes and businesses, and murdered black and white Republican officeholders and political leaders. On election days, armed men at polling places used force to keep blacks from casting ballots.

The 1875 election was especially brutal. In Mississippi armed bands terrorized blacks throughout the state. The worst incident occurred at a Republican campaign barbecue in Clinton where whites murdered thirty blacks, many of them teachers and ministers. Violence in Louisiana was so bad that Governor Adelbert Ames asked President Ulysses S. Grant to send federal troops to protect blacks. The president responded with a curt, one-sentence refusal: "The whole public are tired out with these annual autumnal outbreaks in the south [and] are ready now to condemn any interference on the part of the government."[89] Violence escalated after that because whites knew they would not be punished, and on election day whites even used a cannon to keep blacks away from polling places in Aberdeen. With blacks afraid to vote, Democrats took control of the Louisiana state legislature. The Democrats gave Ames the choice of resigning or being impeached; he quit rather than be disgraced in a mock trial.

Grant's refusal was an indication of the weariness in Northern states over the continuing problems of Reconstruction. That attitude became a major factor in ending Reconstruction.

Northern Indifference and Racism

After ten years of Reconstruction, many Northerners began to resent the federal government's preoccupation with the South. And as Grant noted in denying help to Louisiana, many people were tired of the region's continuing racial violence. Some Northerners were also angry that hundreds of millions of dollars had been spent to help Confederate states recover from the war and to enable freed slaves to begin new lives. Many Northerners believed it was time to quit sheltering the freed slaves, because their rights had been guaranteed by three constitutional amendments. After the Fifteenth Amendment was ratified, a Republican Illinois newspaper that had backed Reconstruction commented: "The negro is now a voter and citizen. Let him hereafter take his chances in the battle of life."[90]

The deep belief Radical Republicans had in racial equality was the moral force that had powered Reconstruction's goal of giving blacks equality. However, this fierce desire for racial justice began to fade as some of the champions of that cause died, left office, or changed their minds about the direction of Reconstruction. The Republican Party also began to grow weaker politically. All of those factors played a part in the political fight over the Civil Rights Act of 1875, the last powerful piece of Reconstruction legislation Congress passed. The final form the bill took showed the waning commitment that Congress had to help blacks and continue interfering in how Southerners governed themselves.

One reason Congress passed the bill on March 1, 1875, was to honor Massachusetts senator Charles Sumner, who had repeatedly

Former state attorney general Robert B. Elliott, standing, delivers a speech on civil rights in January 1874. Elliot was forced to resign his office because of racist politics.

Helpless Against White Political Power

─────────────■─────────────

When whites took full control of state governments after the end of Reconstruction, they removed many black officeholders so that only whites would wield political power. After Wade Hampton was elected South Carolina governor in 1876, he ordered Attorney General Robert B. Elliott to quit. Elliott was forced to leave when the South Carolina Supreme Court sided with Hampton. But in a letter on April 16, 1877, Elliott said it was wrong to force him out:

> We are not insensible to the fact that it is physically competent for the Governor to carry his wishes into effect by [force]. Whilst we shall make no resistance to such a process should he determine to institute it, we trust that the same sense of "responsibility for the proper discharge of the administration" which he pleads as justification for the covert threat of force, will inspire him to pause before taking a step that will obviously trench upon rights guaranteed by that Constitution which he has sworn to obey.

Quoted in Dorothy Sterling, ed., *The Trouble They Seen: Black People Tell the Story of Reconstruction.* New York: Doubleday, 1976, p. 479.

introduced the bill but had died the year before. The legislation prohibited racial discrimination in transportation and public accommodations. Sumner's original measure, however, was weakened by deletion of several other key protections for blacks, including the right to attend white schools. Some Northern congressmen agreed to weaken the bill because of their growing concern that the federal government was gaining too much power over individual states. Even Republican Illinois senator Lyman Trumbull, who backed Reconstruction, had begun to believe that too much federal control would be "destructive at once of the State Governments."[91]

Many congressmen were motivated by legitimate concerns over how rapidly the power of the federal government grew after the Civil War. However, some congressmen also wanted the federal government to quit forcing white Southerners to treat blacks as equals for another reason—they too harbored racist views toward blacks. Although Illinois representative William Richardson had supported abolition of slavery, he had never believed in black equality. He once said, "God made the white man superior to the black, and no legislation will undo or change the decrees of Heaven."[92] Even Trumbull realized that many of his constituents felt that way. He once said that in Illinois, "our people want nothing to do with the negro."[93]

The irony of Reconstruction is that it was imposed on the South by Northern congressmen who were often hypocritical about the issue. The *Independent*, a newspaper that wanted equal rights for blacks, claimed that many Northern lawmakers supported those rights in the South but not in their home states. In an editorial in 1867, the newspaper stated that "when Negro Suffrage is proposed for South Carolina—a Southern State—the Republican party uplifts a lion's paw, and magnificently enforces obedience; but when Negro Suffrage is at issue in Ohio—a Northern State—the Republican party borrows a hare's leg and runs from its own principles."[94] The reason for this is that some congressmen either did not back black rights or represented districts in which most voters were unconcerned about the issue.

In the 1870s Northerners who did not care if blacks had equal rights began to abandon the Republican Party for the Democratic Party. In the 1874 fall elections, Republicans retained control of the Senate, but Democrats won a majority in the U.S. House of Representatives for the first time since 1861. The new Democratic strength was a sign that Reconstruction was in its final days.

The Election That Ended Reconstruction

Democrats gradually began to replace Republicans as the dominant party in Southern states. Democrats won control of Texas in 1873 because the state had more white than black voters. In states with more black voters, whites used violence to bring the Democrats to power. This happened in Alabama in 1874 and Mississippi and Louisiana in 1875. Whites were so brutal in repressing votes in Mississippi that after the election President Grant claimed, "Mississippi is governed today by officials chosen through fraud and violence, such as would scarcely be accredited

Officials count electoral votes during the disputed Tilden-Hayes election. The results from three states were contested, but a special commission determined that Rutherford B. Hayes had won the election.

to savages much less to a civilized and Christian people."[95] The U.S. government, however, did nothing to overturn the results.

By 1876 Democrats believed they could capture the White House for the first time since Abraham Lincoln had been elected in 1860. In the South only Florida, Louisiana, and South Carolina still had Republican governments. The Democratic Party had also gained strength in Northern states. People began voting Democratic because they opposed Reconstruction and blamed Republicans for an economic recession that left many people unemployed.

New York governor Samuel Tilden was the Democratic presidential candidate, and Ohio governor Rutherford B. Hayes was the Republican nominee. On November 7 Tilden garnered nearly 4.3 million votes to just over 4 million for Hayes. Presidents, however, are chosen by electoral votes that each state casts for the candidate who gets the most votes in that state. When the returns were counted, both Republicans and Democrats in Florida, Louisiana, and South Carolina claimed their candidate had won. The results of that political conflict would determine who was president. Congress appointed an electoral commission made up of five senators, five representatives, and five members of the U.S. Supreme Court to settle the dispute. This commission voted 8 to 7 to award the states to Hayes. The decision gave Hayes a 185-to-184 victory in electoral votes.

What looked like a victory for Reconstruction forces, however, was actually a defeat because of a behind-the-scenes political deal

Making Prisoners into Slaves

Many Southern states passed laws when Reconstruction ended that hurt African Americans. In *Forever Free: The Story of Emancipation and Reconstruction*, Eric Foner explains that some new criminal laws were aimed at putting blacks in prison so whites could use them as cheap labor:

> Southern legislatures greatly increased the penalties for petty crimes, a strategy targeted especially against blacks. Mississippi's famous "pig law" defined the theft of any cattle or swine as grand larceny punishable by five years in prison. "They send [a man] to the penitentiary if he steals a chicken," complained a former slave in North Carolina. As the South's prison population rose, the leasing of convicts became a lucrative business. Railroads, mining companies, and other businesses vied for this new form of involuntary labor, the vast majority of them blacks imprisoned for minor offenses. Conditions in labor camps were often barbaric, with disease rife and the death rate high. "One dies, get another" was the motto of the system's architects, since thanks to discriminatory law enforcement by all-white police forces and the exclusion of blacks from juries, there seemed to be an endless supply of black convicts to replace those who perished.

Eric Foner, *Forever Free: The Story of Emancipation and Reconstruction*. New York: Knopf, 2005, p. 202.

the two parties made. In what became known as the Compromise of 1876, Republican leaders agreed to abandon Reconstruction if Democrats on the electoral commission would concede the contested votes to the Republicans. Hayes as president would then allow Democrats to take control of all Southern states. Party officials approved the deal, and the commission on March 2, 1877, awarded the votes to Hayes, who was privately sworn in as president the following day. Two days later, Hayes was inaugurated in a public ceremony.

Hayes predicted blacks would not suffer from the political bargain that made him president. He said he was confident that "absolute justice and fair play to the negro [was possible] by trusting the honorable and influential whites [in the South]."[96] Southern blacks, however, quickly realized what the deal meant for them— that racist whites once again controlled their lives. As former Louisiana slave Henry Adams put it, "The whole South—every state in the South, had got into the hands of the very men that held us as slaves."[97] And those white Southerners began acting immediately to erase the new rights and progress blacks had gained during Reconstruction.

Denying Blacks the Vote

One month after Hayes took office, he made good on the Republican promise to end Reconstruction by ordering the last remaining federal troops in the South to leave Louisiana and South Carolina. They departed on April 10. The election for governor in both states had been disputed. When the soldiers left, Democrats used force to take control of the last two Southern states still governed by Republicans. Hayes then recognized the new governors as legal heads of their states.

On April 11 in South Carolina, Democrat Wade Hampton seized control from Republican governor Daniel H. Chamberlain. One day later, the former Confederate general fired Attorney General Robert B. Elliott and other black officials to ensure that state government was run only by whites. Not all black officials in the South lost their positions in the immediate aftermath of Reconstruction. Blacks continued to vote in Southern states for nearly a generation and were able to elect a few state and national legislators in predominantly black districts.

George H. White, who was born a slave, was a South Carolina state legislator in the 1880s and a U.S. Representative from 1896 to 1901. By the time his final congressional term ended, however, Southern whites had succeeded in taking away the most precious right blacks had—being able to vote. White, the lone black in Congress, complained about that theft in his final House speech on January 29, 1901. He said, "It is an undisputed fact that the negro votes in Alabama, as well as most of the other Southern States, have been effectively suppressed."[98]

Southern states took this right away by passing laws that made it hard for blacks to vote. State legislatures created poll taxes that poor blacks could not afford to pay and literacy tests that most of them flunked because they were also being denied an education in Southern states. The legislatures also created laws that ensured illiterate and poor whites would be able to vote. Whites who could prove their ancestors had voted before 1860, when blacks were still slaves, did not have to pass literacy tests or pay the poll taxes. Election officials also ignored those laws when registering whites who wanted to vote. By the beginning of the twentieth century, only a small number of blacks were still able to vote in Southern states.

Jim Crow

When Louisiana governor Adelbert Ames was forced out of office, he had predicted the takeover of state government by racist whites would be a disaster for blacks. "A race are disenfranchised," he said, "they are to be returned to a condition of serfdom—an era of second slavery."[99] His prophesy came true when blacks lost the right to vote.

The new form of slavery in the post-Reconstruction South did not involve whites owning blacks, but whites had nearly as much power over blacks as they had in the past. By excluding blacks from taking part in government, whites were able to dominate them economically and socially. They were also able to strip blacks of the basic civil liberties the U.S. Constitution guarantees citizens by creating "Jim Crow," a society in which blacks had an inferior status and lived apart from whites.

Under Jim Crow, whites segregated blacks and whites in daily life. Blacks had to travel in separate railroad cars, could not enter

A black man is expelled from a railway car by a white couple.

hotels, restaurants, and places of entertainment used by whites, and even had to use different public toilets. They also had to attend all-black schools, which received less public funding than white schools; they were run down and offered students an inferior education.

Jim Crow violated civil rights blacks had been guaranteed in constitutional amendments approved during Reconstruction. But Southern states were helped in stripping blacks of those rights by several U.S. Supreme Court decisions that denied blacks equality. One of the most devastating decisions was *Plessy v. Ferguson*.

Homer Plessy, a Louisiana black, had claimed his rights to equal protection under the Fourteenth Amendment were violated when he was ejected from a white railroad car. The high court in 1896 ruled that states could create "separate but equal" facilities for blacks and whites. An opinion written by Justice Henry Billings Brown showed how racism influenced the decision. He wrote: "Legislation is powerless to eradicate racial instincts, or to abolish distinctions based upon physical differences. [If] one race be inferior to the other socially, the Constitution of the United States cannot put them on the same plane."[100]

Freed blacks embark for the North on riverboats. Thousands of blacks moved north after the Civil War because of continued discrimination in the South.

That ruling shows how far the federal government had strayed from its goal during Reconstruction of seeking to give blacks equality. That lack of protection made life miserable for Southern blacks for many decades.

"No Home in America"

Life became so bad in the South for blacks that thousands of them moved to Northern states or the western frontier. Some of them even emigrated to Africa. Harrison N. Bouey, a teacher and Baptist minister, organized a group of about two hundred South Carolina blacks who in 1878 sailed for Liberia. Bouey claimed the blacks had no other choice because of how they were being treated. Said Bouey: "The colored man has no home in America. We have no chance to rise from beggars. Men own the capital that we work [and] believe that they still have a right to either us or our value."[101]

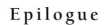

Reconstruction's Bitter Legacy

The Civil Rights battle of the 1960s is sometimes referred to as the Second Reconstruction. It is called that because it was not until then that blacks were able to win back the rights that whites had seized from them when Reconstruction ended. One of that decade's most memorable events occurred on August 28, 1963, when a quarter million people marched in Washington, D.C., to protest the racism that still denied blacks their rights.

The highlight of that historic day was when Reverend Martin Luther King Jr. addressed the huge crowd gathered at the Lincoln Memorial. King spoke eloquently about his dream that the United States would one day become a nation in which all people were treated equally. He began by noting that a century after President Abraham Lincoln issued the Emancipation Proclamation, African Americans had still not achieved equality. Said King:

> But one hundred years later, the Negro still is not free. One hundred years later, the life of the Negro is still sadly crippled by the manacles of segregation and the chains of discrimination. One hundred years later, the Negro lives on a lonely island of poverty in the midst of a vast ocean

Martin Luther King Jr. addresses a crowd outside the Lincoln Memorial in 1963. The civil rights protests of the 1960s are sometimes called the "Second Reconstruction."

of material prosperity. One hundred years later, the Negro is still languishing in the corners of American society and finds himself an exile in his own land.[102]

For a brief period during Reconstruction, blacks had come close to realizing King's dream of true freedom and equality. The tragedy of Reconstruction was that its failure denied blacks that dream for another century.

A Century of Black Repression

From the end of Reconstruction until the civil rights triumphs of the 1960s, Southern whites dominated blacks almost as completely as they had during slavery. Blacks were no longer slaves, but their freedom was limited by all-white government and judicial systems that denied them rights like being able to vote and sit on juries and barred them from many restaurants, hotels, and other public facilities.

In addition to this official repression, racist whites continued to use violence to make blacks fear and obey them. The physical brutality whites employed became so widespread that it got its own name—lynching. Originally in the United States, lynching meant the unauthorized punishment of a person for a crime, such as a murderer who was hanged without a trial. But Southern whites killed so many blacks after Reconstruction that lynching came to mean the murder of a black person. The Tuskegee Institute, which kept lynching records, reports that whites killed 3,445 blacks from 1882 through 1968. They usually murdered blacks by hanging them, often in brutal public exhibitions before hundreds or even thousands of people, but they also shot, burned, beat, and tortured them to death.

Most blacks were lynched because they tried to exercise civil rights like voting, refused to let whites bully them in their daily

Dates Former Confederate States Were Readmitted to the Union

Tennessee	July 24, 1866
Arkansas	June 22, 1868
Florida	June 25, 1868
North Carolina	July 4, 1868
South Carolina	July 9, 1868
Louisiana	July 9, 1868
Alabama	July 13, 1868
Virginia	January 26, 1870
Mississippi	February 23, 1870
Texas	March 30, 1870
Georgia	July 15, 1870

lives, or were successful in business. When several blacks were killed in Memphis, Tennessee, in 1882, Frederick Douglass claimed whites murdered them because they were good businessmen. Douglass said that was a common excuse for lynching blacks:

> The men lynched at Memphis were murdered because they were prosperous. They were doing a business which a white firm desired to do—hence the mob and hence the murder. When a negro is degraded and ignorant he conforms to a popular standard of what a Negro should be.

An angry mob lynches a black man. Whites used lynching to keep blacks from exercising their basic civil rights.

When he shakes off his rags and wretchedness and presumes to be a man [he] contradicts this popular standard and becomes an offence to [whites].[103]

The combination of governmental and physical subjugation forced Southern blacks to endure Jim Crow for decades. Blyden Jackson, who wrote novels and taught Southern literature at the University of North Carolina, once explained what it was like growing up in Louisville, Kentucky, in the early twentieth century. "I knew," he said simply, "that there were two Louisvilles and two Americas."[104] The white Louisville had fancy restaurants, hotels, and theaters blacks could never enter. People in white Louisville generally lived in nice homes, received a good education, and had decent jobs. Residents of black Louisville mostly lived in run-down homes or apartments, rarely went to school, and worked at low-paying, menial jobs. They were also subjected to racist abuse on a daily basis in their contact with private citizens as well as police officers and other government officials.

This pattern was the same in other Southern communities after Reconstruction, including Atlanta, Georgia, where Martin Luther King Jr. was born. By the time he was a high school student, King knew blacks would never have equality until the nation enforced the intent of the amendments added to the U.S. Constitution during Reconstruction. In a speech titled "The Negro and the Constitution," for which King won a national contest, he said: "[The nation during Reconstruction passed three] amendments making it the fundamental law that thenceforth there should be no discrimination anywhere in the 'land of the free' [and] today thirteen million black sons and daughters of our forefathers continue the fight for the translation of the 13th, 14th, and 15th amendments from writing on the printed page to an actuality."[105]

King led the fight that made the federal government honor those promises. The result was that blacks finally gained equality with whites and protection from white violence.

Reconstruction's Living Legacy

The past injustices done to African Americans still haunt many people today. The Virginia General Assembly in February 2007 voted unanimously to apologize for slavery and the racist way Virginia residents and the state had treated blacks for a century afterward. The resolution labeled that treatment "the most horrendous of all depredations of human rights and violations of our founding ideals in our nation's history."[106] Virginia's apology led several other states like Georgia and even the federal government to consider making similar amends to African Americans.

One reason some people think such apologies are in order is that those past injustices still affect blacks today. Edward DuBose, president of the Georgia State Conference of the National Association for the Advancement of Colored People, said in March 2007 that it is important to understand how past treatment that denied blacks opportunities to become educated and successful are affecting their descendants today. He said the question that needs to be asked is, "To what extent are African Americans still second-class citizens [because of past racism]?"[107] Thus Reconstruction is not a meaningless event confined to history books but a living reality that has shaped the way many people live today.

Notes

Introduction: A Nation Divided by War and Race

1. Quoted in Robert Kelley, *The Shaping of the American Past*. Englewood Cliffs, NJ: Prentice Hall, p. 856.

2. Quoted in William Loren Katz, *Eyewitness: The Negro in American History*. New York: Pittman, 1971, p. 50.

3. Frederick Douglass, *Autobiographies: Narrative of the Life of Frederick Douglass, an American Slave*. New York: Library of America, 1984, p. 400.

4. Quoted in Katz, *Eyewitness*, p. 112.

5. Quoted in Kelley, *The Shaping of the American Past*, p. 320.

6. Quoted in Stephen B. Oates, *With Malice Toward None: The Life of Abraham Lincoln*. New York: Harper and Row, 1977, p. 143.

7. Quoted in Paul M. Angle, ed., *The Lincoln Reader*. New Brunswick, NJ: Rutgers University Press, 1947, p. 402.

8. Quoted in Samuel Eliot Morison, *The Oxford History of the American People*. New York: Oxford University Press, 1965, p. 653.

9. Avery Craven, *Reconstruction: The Ending of the Civil War*. New York: Holt, Rinehart and Winston, 1969, p. 2.

10. Quoted in Eric Foner, *Forever Free: The Story of Emancipation and Reconstruction*. New York: Knopf, 2005, p. 67.

Chapter 1: The Political Fight for Reconstruction

11. Quoted in Morison, *The Oxford History of the American People*, p. 702.

12. Quoted in John Hope Franklin, *Reconstruction: After the Civil War*. Chicago: University of Chicago Press, 1961, p. 54.

13. Quoted in Oates, *With Malice Toward None*, p. 431.

14. Quoted in Hodding Carter, *The Angry Scar: The Story of Reconstruction*. New York: Doubleday, 1959, p. 44.

15. Quoted in Foner, *Forever Free*, p. 109.

16. Quoted in Dorothy Sterling, ed., *The Trouble They Seen: Black People Tell the Story of Reconstruction*. New York: Doubleday, 1976, p. 66.

17. Quoted in Craven, *Reconstruction*, p. 128.

18. Quoted in David Brion Davis, *Inhuman Bondage: The Rise and Fall of Slavery in the New World*. New York: Oxford University Press, 2006, p. 319.

19. Quoted in *The History Place: Abraham Lincoln*, "Speech on Reconstruction." www.historyplace.com/lincoln/reconst.html.

20. Quoted in Craven, *Reconstruction*, p. 140.

21. Quoted in Claude G. Bowers, *The Tragic Era: The Revolution After Lincoln*. Cambridge, MA: Houghton Mifflin, 1929, p. 108.

22. Quoted in Foner, *Forever Free*, p. 116.

23. Quoted in Lerone Bennett Jr., *Black Power U.S.A.: The Human Side of Reconstruction, 1867–1877*. Chicago: Johnson, 1967, p. 41.

24. Quoted in Calvin D. Linton, ed., *The Bicentennial Almanac*. New York: Regency, 1975, p. 196.

25. Quoted in Craven, *Reconstruction*, p. 217.

26. Quoted in Eric Foner, *Reconstruction: America's Unfinished Revolution, 1863–1877*. New York: Harper and Row, 1989, p. 334.

27. Quoted in Linton, *The Bicentennial Almanac*, p. 197.

Chapter 2: From Slavery to Freedom

28. Quoted in Davis, *Inhuman Bondage*, p. 298.

29. Quoted in Davis, *Inhuman Bondage*, p. 298.

30. Quoted in Foner, *Forever Free*, p. 78.

31. Quoted in Carter, *The Angry Scar*, p. 49.

32. Quoted in Spencer Crew, Cynthia Goodman, and Henry Louis Gates, *Unchained Memories: Readings from the Slave Narratives*. Boston: Bulfinch, 2002, p. 149.

33. Quoted in Foner, *Forever Free*, p. 42.

34. Quoted in Foner, *Forever Free*, p. 43.

35. Quoted in James Oliver Horton and Lois E. Horton, *Slavery and the Making of America*. New York: Oxford University Press, 2005, p. 197.

36. Quoted in Katz, *Eyewitness*, p. 210.

37. Quoted in Norman Yetman, ed., *Voices from Slavery*. New York; Holt, Rinehart and Winston, 1970, p. 183.

38. Quoted in Kenneth M. Stampp and Leon F. Litwack, eds., *Reconstruction: An Anthology of Revisionist Writing*. Baton Rouge: Louisiana State University Press, 1969, p. 194.

39. Quoted in Crew et al., *Unchained Memories*, p. 152.

40. Quoted in Carter, *The Angry Scar*, p. 49.

41. Quoted in Yetman, *Voices from Slavery*, p. 138.

42. Quoted in Katz, *Eyewitness*, p. 242.

43. Quoted in Katz, *Eyewitness*, p. 242.

44. Quoted in Stampp and Litwack, *Reconstruction*, p. 108.

45. Quoted in Sterling, *The Trouble They Seen*, p. 27.

46. Quoted in Foner, *Forever Free*, p. 82.

Chapter 3: Fighting for Equality with Whites

47. Quoted in Foner, *Forever Free*, p. 128.

48. Quoted in Bowers, *The Tragic Era*, p. 114.

49. Quoted in Craven, *Reconstruction*, p. 235.

50. Quoted in Stampp and Litwack, *Reconstruction*, p. 463.

51. Quoted in Franklin, *Reconstruction*, p. 105.

52. Quoted in Franklin, *Reconstruction*, p. 105.

53. Quoted in Katz, *Eyewitness*, p. 243.

54. Quoted in Foster Rhea Dulles, *The United States Since 1865*. Ann Arbor: University of Michigan Press, 1971, p. 25.

55. Quoted in Morison, *The Oxford History of the American People*, p. 723.

56. Quoted in Sterling, *The Trouble They Seen*, p. 139.

57. Quoted in Yetman, *Voices from Slavery*, p. 241.

58. Quoted in Dorothy Schneider and Carl J. Schneider, *An Eyewitness History: Slavery in America from Colonial Times to the Civil War*. New York: Facts On File, 2000, p. 340.

59. Quoted in Sterling, *The Trouble They Seen*, p. 262.

60. Quoted in Katz, *Eyewitness*, p. 242.

61. Quoted in Yetman, *Voices from Slavery*, p. 315.

62. Quoted in Foner, *Forever Free*, p. 202.

63. Quoted in Franklin, *Reconstruction*, p. 87.

Chapter 4: Southern Whites Oppose Reconstruction

64. Quoted in Bennett, *Black Power U.S.A.*, p. 25.

65. Walter White, *Rope and Faggot: A Biography of Judge Lynch*. New York: Arno, 1969, p. 95.

66. James Elbert Cutler, *Lynch-Law: An Investigation into the History of Lynching in the United States*. New York: Longmans, Green, 1905, p. 153.

67. Quoted in Philip Dray, *At the Hands of Persons Unknown: The Lynching of Black America*. New York: Random House, 2002, p. 37.

68. Quoted in Katz, *Eyewitness*, p. 252.

69. Quoted in Foner, *Forever Free*, p. 38.

70. Quoted in Dray, *At the Hands of Persons Unknown*, p. 43.

71. Quoted in Schneider and Schneider, *An Eyewitness History*, p. 323.

72. Quoted in Katz, *Eyewitness*, p. 280.

73. Quoted in Sterling, *The Trouble They Seen*, p. 378.

74. Quoted in Katz, *Eyewitness*, p. 267.

75. Quoted in Craven, *Reconstruction*, p. 60.

76. Quoted in Yetman, *Voices from Slavery*, p. 38.

77. Quoted in Sterling, *The Trouble They Seen*, p. 369.

78. Quoted in Dray, *At the Hands of Persons Unknown*, p. 45.

79. Quoted in Yetman, *Voices from Slavery*, p. 303.

80. Quoted in Foner, *Reconstruction*, p. 342.

81. Quoted in Foner, *Forever Free*, p. 134.

82. Quoted in Katz, *Eyewitness*, p. 267.

83. Quoted in Milton Meltzer, ed., *The Black Americans: A History in Their Own Words, 1619-1983*. New York: Thomas Y. Crowell, 1984, p. 94.

84. Quoted in Foner, *Reconstruction*, p. 437.

85. Quoted in Sterling, *The Trouble They Seen*, p. 375.

Chapter 5: The End of Reconstruction and Equal Rights

86. Quoted in Foner, *Forever Free*, p. 148.

87. Quoted in Franklin, *Reconstruction*, p. 107.

88. Quoted in Bennett, *Black Power U.S.A.*, p. 356.

89. Quoted in Morison, *The Oxford History of the American People*, p. 724.

90. Quoted in Bennett, *Black Power U.S.A.*, p. 367.

91. Quoted in Franklin, *Reconstruction*, p. 199.

92. Quoted in Craven, *Reconstruction*, p. 263.

93. Quoted in Davis, *Inhuman Bondage*, p. 312.

94. Quoted in Craven, *Reconstruction*, p. 266.

95. Quoted in Bennett, *Black Power U.S.A.*, p. 369.

96. Quoted in Katz, *Eyewitness*, p. 252.

97. Quoted in Foner, *Reconstruction*, p. 582.

98. Quoted in *Documents of the American South*, "Defense of the Negro Race—Charges Answered. Speech of Hon. George H. White, of North Carolina, in the House of Representatives, January 29, 1901." http://docsouth.unc.edu/nc/white gh/whitegh.html.

99. Quoted in Bennett, *Black Power U.S.A.*, p. 367.

100. Quoted in Dray, *At the Hands of Persons Unknown*, p. 111.

101. Quoted in Foner, *Forever Free*, p. 199.

Epilogue: Reconstruction's Bitter Legacy

102. Quoted in Avalon Project at Yale Law School, "I Have a Dream by Martin Luther King, Jr.; August 28, 1963." www.yale.edu/lawweb/avalon/treatise/king/mlk01.html.

103. Quoted in Anne P. Rice, ed., *Witnessing Lynching: American Writers Respond*. New Brunswick, NJ: Rutgers University Press, 2003, p. 41.

104. Quoted in Foner, *Forever Free*, p. 212.

105. Quoted in AFRO-American Almanac, "The Negro and the Constitution by Martin L. King Jr." www.toptags.com/aama/voices/speeches/negrocon.html.

106. Quoted in Associated Press, "Virginia Lawmakers Apologize for Slavery," *Milwaukee Journal Sentinel*, February 25, 2007, p. A3.

107. Quoted in Jenny Jarvis, "Slavery Apologies Debated Across the U.S.," *Los Angeles Times*, March 19, 2007, p. B1.

Chronology

January 1, 1863 President Abraham Lincoln signs the Emancipation Proclamation to free slaves in Confederate states.

December 8, 1863 President Lincoln announces the Proclamation of Amnesty and Reconstruction.

March 3, 1865 Congress establishes the Bureau of Refugees, Freedmen, and Abandoned Lands.

April 9, 1865 The Confederate States of America surrenders to end the Civil War.

April 14, 1865 President Lincoln is shot while attending a play; he dies the next morning. Vice President Andrew Johnson becomes president.

December 6, 1865 The Thirteenth Amendment is ratified.

April 9, 1866 Congress overrides President Andrew Johnson's veto to pass the Civil Rights Bill.

July 30, 1866 A race riot occurs in New Orleans.

March 2, 1867 The First Reconstruction Act becomes law.

March 4, 1868 President Andrew Johnson's impeachment trial begins.

July 9, 1868 The Fourteenth Amendment is ratified

March 4, 1869 Ulysses Grant is inaugurated as the eighteenth president of the United States.

February 3, 1870 The Fifteenth Amendment is ratified.

February 25, 1870 Hiram R. Revels of Mississippi becomes the first African American to take a seat in the U.S. Senate.

November 5, 1873 President Grant is reelected.

March 1, 1875 Congress passes the Civil Rights Act.

November 7, 1876 The presidential election between Republican Rutherford B. Hayes and Democrat Samuel Tilden is disputed.

March 5, 1877 Rutherford Hayes is publicly sworn in as the nineteenth president of the United States.

April 10, 1877 The last Union troops withdraw from South Carolina.

For Further Reading

Books

Tonya Bolden, *Cause: Reconstruction America, 1863–1877*. New York: Knopf Books for Young Readers, 2005. An informative book for younger readers that has many good photographs from the period.

William Edward Burghardt Du Bois, *Black Reconstruction in America*. New York: Atheneum, 1992. A reprint of the 1935 book by this prominent African American historian, writer, and civil rights leader.

William Dudley, ed., *Reconstruction*. San Diego: Greenhaven, 2003. A series of essays on issues and events during Reconstruction.

Eric Foner and Olivia Mahoney, *America's Reconstruction: People and Politics After the Civil War*. New York: Harper-Perennial, 1995. A scholarly, informative treatment of this period.

Meg Greene, *Into the Land of Freedom: African Americans in Reconstruction*. Minneapolis: Lerner, 2004. A thorough study of the period for younger readers.

Wilbert L. Jenkins, *Climbing Up to Glory: A Short History of African Americans During the Civil War and Reconstruction*. Wilmington, DE: SR, 2002. A solid account of what happened to African Americans during Reconstruction.

Dorothy Schneider and Carl J. Schneider, *An Eyewitness History: Slavery in America from Colonial Times to the Civil War*. New York: Checkmark, 2000. Great pictures, time lines, eyewitness accounts, and key documents.

Web Sites

American Experience: Reconstruction: The Second Civil War, PBS (www. pbs. org/wgbh/amex/reconstruction/ index.html). This Web site based on a Public Broadcasting Service program telecast in 2004 has detailed information on Reconstruction.

America's Reconstruction: People and Politics After the Civil War, Digital History (www.digitalhistory.uh.edu/ reconstruction/index.html). Text by historians Eric Foner and Olivia Mahoney plus pictures, documents, and narratives from the period.

Black History Pages (www.blackhistory pages.com). This Web site has links to the best Web sites on lynching and other aspects of African American history.

Civil War and Reconstruction, 1861– 1877, Library of Congress (www. memory. loc.gov/learn/features/time line/civilwar/recon/reconone.html). This federal government Web site has images, documents, and first person accounts of Reconstruction.

Index

Picture Credits

Cover: © CORBIS

Private Collection/Peter Newark American Pictures/
The Bridgeman Art Library, 31, 34

Drawing by Frank Bellew, Harper's Weekly, 65

© Bettmann/CORBIS, 13, 24, 27, 39, 44, 88

© CORBIS, 72

The Bridgeman Art Library/Getty Images, 82

Hulton Archive/Getty Images, 36, 57, 86

Time Life Pictures/Getty Images, 52

Library of Congress, 9, 18, 23, 48, 51, 75

National Archives and Records Administration, 11

North Wind Picture Archives, 19, 33, 41, 46, 49, 56,
63, 67, 78, 83

About the Author

Michael V. Uschan has written more than sixty books, including *Life of an American Soldier in Iraq*, for which he won the 2005 Council for Wisconsin Writers Juvenile Nonfiction Award. It was the second time he won the award. Mr. Uschan began his career as a writer and editor with United Press International, a wire service that provided stories to newspapers, radio, and television. Journalism is sometimes called "history in a hurry." Mr. Uschan considers writing history books a natural extension of the skills he developed in his many years as a journalist. He and his wife Barbara reside in the Milwaukee suburb of Franklin, Wisconsin.